The Apology

and Related Dialogues

The Apology

and Related Dialogues

Plato

Edited and Introduced by Andrew Bailey

Translated by Cathal Woods and Ryan Pack

broadview press

BROADVIEW PRESS – www.broadviewpress.com
Peterborough, Ontario, Canada

Founded in 1985, Broadview Press remains a wholly independent publishing house. Broadview's focus is on academic publishing; our titles are accessible to university and college students as well as scholars and general readers. With over 600 titles in print, Broadview has become a leading international publisher in the humanities, with world-wide distribution. Broadview is committed to environmentally responsible publishing and fair business practices.

The interior of this book is printed on 100% recycled paper.

Library and Archives Canada Cataloguing in Publication

Plato
[Dialogues. Selections. English]
    The Apology and related dialogues / Plato ; edited and introduced by Andrew Bailey ; translated by Cathal Woods and Ryan Pack.

Includes bibliographical references and index.
ISBN 978-1-55481-258-5 (paperback)

    1. Socrates. I. Bailey, Andrew, 1969–, editor
II. Woods, Cathal, translator III. Pack, Ryan, translator
IV. Title. V. Title: Dialogues. Selections. English

B365.A5W65 2016   184   C2016-900850-9

Broadview Press handles its own distribution in North America
PO Box 1243, Peterborough, Ontario K9J 7H5, Canada
555 Riverwalk Parkway, Tonawanda, NY 14150, USA
Tel: (705) 743-8990; Fax: (705) 743-8353
email: customerservice@broadviewpress.com

Distribution is handled by Eurospan Group in the UK, Europe, Central Asia, Middle East, Africa, India, Southeast Asia, Central America, South America, and the Caribbean. Distribution is handled by Footprint Books in Australia and New Zealand.

Broadview Press acknowledges the financial support of the Government of Canada through the Canada Book Fund for our publishing activities.

Copy-edited by Martin R. Boyne

Typesetting and assembly: True to Type Inc., Claremont, Canada
Cover Design: Lisa Brawn

PRINTED IN CANADA

Contents

Socrates

Plato

Introduction

Who Were Plato and Socrates?

Plato

The historical details of Plato's life are somewhat obscure, though we know more about his life than about the lives of most ancient philosophers and he is the first whose entire body of philosophical work survives. He is traditionally thought to have been born in about 427 BCE and to have died in 347. His family, who lived in the Greek city-state of Athens, was aristocratic and probably wealthy. Legend has it that Plato's father, Ariston, was descended from Codrus, the last king of Athens. His mother, Perictione, was related to the great Solon, who around 570 BCE had completely reformed the notoriously harsh Athenian legal system laid out by Draco in the seventh century, and replaced the hereditary aristocracy with a citizenship whose ranks were based on wealth. Solon's reforms were considered to have removed conditions that might otherwise have led to civil war and tyranny. When democracy was introduced in Athens, in the fifth century BCE, Solon's constitution provided the basis from which the new constitution grew.

While Plato was still a boy his father died, and his mother married Pyrilampes, a friend of the revered Athenian statesman Pericles, who in the 450s had transformed Athens into one of the greatest cities in the Greek world. As a young man Plato fought with the Athenian army against Sparta during the Peloponnesian War (431–404)—which Athens lost—and he may have served again around 395 when Athens was involved in the Corinthian War (395–386).

Given his family connections, Plato seemed set to play a prominent role in Athenian political life, and, as it happened, when he was about 23 a political revolution occurred in Athens that could have catapulted him into public affairs. The coup swept the previous democratic rulers—who had just lost the war against Sparta—out of power and into exile and replaced them with the so-called Thirty Tyrants, several of whom were friends and relatives of Plato: two of these, Critias and Charmides, appear in his dialogues. It seems that Plato, an idealistic young man, expected that this revolution would usher in a new era of justice and good government, but he was soon disillusioned; the new regime proved to be even more violent and corrupt than the old. He withdrew from public life in disgust.

The rule of the Thirty lasted only about nine months, and soon afterwards the exiled democrats were restored to power. Plato—impressed by the newly restored leaders' lenience toward the coup leaders—apparently thought again about entering politics. But then, in 399 BCE, the prosecution and conviction of his old friend and mentor Socrates caused him again to change his mind. Plato, along with some other philosophical followers of Socrates, fled Athens and went west to the city of Megara to stay with the philosopher Eucleides (a follower of the great Greek philosopher Parmenides of Elea). He may also have visited Egypt, though his travels at this time are shrouded in myth. It appears that Plato started writing in earnest at about this time; certainly, the earliest writings that have come down to us date from this point.

Almost all of Plato's writings are in the form of dialogues between two or more characters, and in most of them the character that takes the leading role in the discussion is Socrates. Writing in the dialogue form was not unique to Plato; for example, a friend of Socrates, the general Xenophon, wrote a number of dialogues that provide another major source for Socrates' life. Plato, though, was by far the greatest practitioner of the dialogue form. Since Plato never wrote himself into any of his dialogues, it is often—though not uncontroversially—assumed that the views expressed by the character of Socrates more or less correspond with those that Plato is trying to put forward.

When Plato was about 40, he made another trip away from Athens, visiting Italy to talk with the Pythagorean philosophers who lived there, and traveling to Syracuse on the island of Sicily. There, during a long stay, he became close friends with Dion, the brother-in-law of the ruling tyrant Dionysius I. Dion became Plato's pupil and (according to legend) came to prefer a philosophical life of moral goodness to the pleasure, luxury, and power of his surroundings. Exactly what happened next is unclear, but there is some reason to believe that Plato was captured by a displeased Dionysius and sold into slavery, and that he was rescued from the slave market only by having his freedom purchased by a member of a different philosophical school influenced by Socrates (the Cyrenaics).

On Plato's return to Athens he bought some land in the precinct named for an Athenian hero called Academus, and there, in about 385 BCE, he founded the first European research center (or, at least, the

first of which there is any real historical knowledge). Because of its lo-
cation this school was called the Academy; it was to remain in exis-
tence for more than 900 years, until 529 CE. For most of the rest of his
life, Plato stayed at the Academy, directing its studies. Very quickly,
the school became a vital center for research in all kinds of subjects,
both theoretical and practical: it was probably one of the first cradles
for the study of metaphysics, epistemology, psychology, ethics, politics, aesthetics, and mathematical science, and members were invited
by various Greek city-states to help draft new political constitutions.
All known mathematicians of the fourth century had links to the Academy. Theaetetus of Athens and Eudoxus of Cnidus, together with
Plato's Italian friend Archytas of Tarentum, helped to develop the
mathematics that form the latter part of Euclid's *Elements*.

In 368, Dionysius I of Sicily died and Dion persuaded his succes-
sor, Dionysius II, to send for Plato so that the latter could advise him
on how the state should be run. Plato, who was now about 60, agreed
to go, albeit with some misgivings; possibly he hoped to make the
younger Dionysius an example of a philosopher-king and to put his
own political doctrines into practice. If so, the experiment was a dis-
astrous failure, as Dion was soon sent into exile and Plato effectively
held prisoner by Dionysius. After returning to Athens for a few years,
Plato once again traveled to Sicily, at the urging of both Dion and
Dionysius, and was again taken prisoner. In 360, he was finally able
to escape and return to Athens for good. He died thirteen years later,
at the ripe age of 80.

Socrates

Socrates was Plato's primary intellectual influence: though he left no
writings, Socrates' personality and ideas were so powerful that he appears to have had a tremendous impact upon everyone he encountered,
inspiring either intense devotion or powerful irritation. Born in about 470
BCE, Socrates would have been in his late 50s when a teenaged Plato fell
under his influence, and he was about 70 when he was executed.

Socrates' father was a sculptor and his mother a midwife, and he
initially earned his living as a stonemason. He married a much younger
woman, Xanthippe, who bore him three sons. Little is known about
the historical Xanthippe, but she has become a byword for spirited,
argumentative women, and Socrates is depicted, in a dialogue written
by another of his students, Xenophon, as saying that this fiery personality is why he married her.

Like Plato, Socrates served valiantly as a soldier—an infantry-
man—in the Athenian army during the ongoing wars with Sparta and
its allies. Like all Athenian citizens he was also occasionally involved

in civic politics, acting for a period as an overseer of the council of citizens appointed to run daily affairs of the city (the *boule*); however, in general Socrates steered clear of political life.

He lived very simply—some of his contemporaries thought, with ostentatious and unnecessary poverty—and was known for going barefoot even during bitterly cold weather. He was the butt of jokes, in which he often shared with apparent good humor, for his ugliness; he was short, with bandy legs—giving him a swaggering walk—a snub nose, bulging eyes, bristling eyebrows, and a paunch.

Socrates' main philosophical concern was the ethical question of how one's life should best be lived, and his method was to engage in systematic cross-examination (*elenchus*) of those he encountered, challenging them to state and then to justify their own beliefs about justice and virtue. Socrates frequently demonstrated to his conversants that their critically unconsidered beliefs about moral virtue were self-contradictory and hence that those beliefs *had* no justification. The state of bewildered awareness of their own ignorance in which Socrates left his unfortunate victims is called *aporia*, and Socrates' technique of remorseless questioning is sometimes known as the "aporetic method."

Though Socrates was famous for insisting that he was wiser than his fellow Athenians only because he alone realized that he knew nothing, he did subscribe to a handful of substantive philosophical positions, two of which in particular he passed on to Plato. First, for Socrates, virtue (*arete*) is a kind of knowledge: that is, to be a virtuous person is, fundamentally, to *understand* what the good—the right thing to do—is, in much the same way as being an expert shoemaker consists in knowing everything there is to know about shoes. Socrates (and Plato after him) therefore held that it was vitally important to find correct definitions—or to understand the essence (*eidos*)—of ethical concepts; otherwise, we will not know how to live. In this way, ethical research would parallel mathematical research, in which the researcher tries to establish definitions for fundamental objects and then to prove results about those objects.

Wisdom is sufficient for virtue, Socrates thought, because no one does the wrong thing on purpose. We always desire to do what is best for us; it's just that sometimes we fail to understand what is in our own best interests. Every departure from moral virtue is a failure of wisdom—a failure, simply, to understand what is the right thing to do.

The second crucial Socratic doctrine is that the real essence of a person is not the body but the soul, and that this soul is immortal: the health of one's own soul is thus of paramount importance and is far more significant than the mere slings and arrows of physical life. Indeed, Socrates was convinced that, even while we are living in the physical world, the quality of our souls is a far more important determinant of our happiness than external circumstances like health, wealth, popularity, or power.

Socrates' goal, then, was the "care of the soul"—making one's soul as good and healthy as possible. And he thought that he had a mission, commanded by the god Apollo, to try to improve the souls of his fellow Athenians as well. This burnishing of the soul comes down to becoming as *wise* as possible—all virtue follows from wisdom, and it is wisdom that gives everything else, such as health and wealth, its value. What is the point of having money, for example, if you do not know what to do with it? The pursuit of wisdom requires questioning convention—refusing to do or believe things merely because they are expected or traditional—and committing oneself only to what is rationally justified. As Plato has Socrates famously put it in the *Apology*, the unexamined life is not worth living. Potentially, therefore, Socrates' philosophy is revolutionary. He was clear, too, that the point of examining one's presuppositions is not merely to come to possess more correct *beliefs*; it is to learn how one should *act* in life. The expression of a healthy soul is appropriate behavior.

Although wisdom is a kind of knowledge, it is not something that can be taught, in the standard sense of having things described or explained to you. Each individual must come to wisdom by grappling *themselves* with important ideas, such as justice, piety, courage, or balance. Here is one way to think of this. The nature of piety, for example, is to be understood by grasping the essence of *piety*—to put it a little anachronistically, it is a concept, and what it is to grasp a concept is to be able to define it. However, merely being able to rhyme off the definition is not adequate—it is not genuine understanding. Real grasp of the concept involves knowing *why* it is the way it is—why other ways of defining it are wrong, not just because some convention says so but because these *could not* be the way piety is. The aim of the Socratic method is to push people into thinking for themselves and performing the difficult mental activity that is the only way of coming to the genuine understanding of key concepts that constitutes knowledge of virtue.

As the Roman philosopher Cicero put it, more than 300 years after Socrates' death, "Socrates was the first to call philosophy down from the heavens and to place it in cities, and even to introduce it into homes and compel it to inquire about human life, ethical conduct, and goods and evils."[1] Though Socrates found many sympathetic students among

---

1   *Tusculan Disputations* vol. 10, c. 45 BCE.

the youth of Athens, his often antagonistic rhetorical methods and his questioning of commonly held Athenian beliefs was not appreciated by all. In 399 BCE, three citizens brought trumped-up charges against Socrates, accusing him of impiety toward the city's gods and of corrupting the youth of Athens. It is not clear how far this prosecution was inspired by political opposition to Socrates, who had associated with members of the Thirty Tyrants, among others. Socrates was convicted by the majority of a jury of 500 citizens and—since he declared that he would rather die than give up philosophy (even though he would probably not have been executed had he chosen exile as a penalty)—he was executed by being given a poison, hemlock, to drink.

What Was Plato's Overall Philosophical Project?

Although the following dialogues, like nearly all of Plato's work, feature Socrates as their main protagonist, it is important to bear in mind that these dialogues were written by Plato, not Socrates—indeed, they were written after Socrates' death—and are expressions of *Plato's* philosophy, although undoubtedly Plato was heavily influenced by Socrates and had many very similar views, especially at the time these dialogues were written.

Plato is often regarded as the inventor of Western philosophy—and with some justification. His thought encompassed nearly all of the areas that are central to philosophy today—including metaphysics, epistemology, ethics, political theory, aesthetics, and the philosophy of science and mathematics—and for the first time in European history dealt with them in a unified way.[1] Plato thought of philosophy as a special discipline with its own intellectual method, and he was convinced that it had an absolutely foundational importance in human life. Only philosophy, Plato thought, could provide genuine understanding, since only philosophy scrutinized the assumptions that other disciplines left unquestioned. Furthermore, according to Plato, philosophy reveals a realm of comprehensive and unitary hidden truths—indeed, a whole level of reality that is undetectable by the senses—which goes far beyond everyday common sense and which, when properly understood, has the power to revolutionize how we live our lives and organize our societies. Philosophy, and only philosophy, holds the key to genuine human happiness and well-being.

---

1   In fact the mathematician and philosopher Alfred North Whitehead (1861–1947) famously was moved to say, "The safest general characterization of the European philosophical tradition is that it consists of a series of footnotes to Plato."

This realm of objects that Plato claimed to have discovered is generally known as the Platonic Forms. The Forms, according to Plato, are changeless, eternal objects that lie outside of both the physical world and the minds of individuals, and they can be encountered only through pure thought (rather than by the senses). One of Plato's favorite examples of a Form is the mathematical property of Equality. In the *Phaedo* he argues that Equality itself cannot be identical with two equal sticks, or with any other group of physical objects of equal length, since we could always be mistaken about whether any two observed objects are really equal with one another, but we could not possibly be mistaken about Equality itself and somehow take *it* to be unequal. When two sticks are equal in length, therefore, they "participate in" Equality—it is their relation to Equality that makes them equal rather than unequal—but Equality itself is an abstract object that exists over and above all the instances of equal things. The Form of Equality is what one succeeds in understanding when one has a proper conception of what equality really is in itself: real knowledge, therefore, comes not from observation but from acquaintance with the Forms. Other central examples of Forms, for Plato, are Sameness, Number, Motion, Beauty, Justice, Piety, and (the most important Form of all) Goodness.

The relation of the ordinary world of perceivable, concrete objects to the realm of the Forms is described by Plato in Book VII of one of his major works, the *Republic*, using the allegory of a cave. Ordinary people, lacking the benefit of a philosophical education, are like prisoners trapped since birth in an underground cave and forced to look only at shadows cast on the wall in front of them by puppets behind their backs, dancing in front of a fire. With the proper philosophical encouragement, they can—if they have the courage to do so—break their bonds and turn around to see that what they believed was reality itself was really only an illusory puppet show. The philosophers among them can even leave the cave and there they will encounter the true reality—of which even the puppets are only copies—illuminated by the light of the sun, which, for Plato, represents the Form of the Good. The perceptible world is thus merely an imperfect image of—and is sustained by—the quasi-divine, eternal realm of the unchanging and unobservable Forms.

What Is the Structure of These Dialogues?

The dialogues collected here are some of the first works Plato wrote: the *Apology*, *Crito*, and *Euthyphro* were probably written sometime between 399 and 387 BCE—that is, in the years immediately following the death of Socrates, when Plato was in his late 20s and 30s. The *Phaedo* was likely written sometime later and is part of a sequence of dialogues in which the mature Plato moves away from the views of Socrates and develops ideas that depart significantly from what Socrates taught (even though he still uses Socrates as the main protagonist in these dialogues). However, the only part of the *Phaedo* included here is Socrates' death scene, so it is reasonable to treat all the works collected here as representative of the "early" Plato, in which—it is generally agreed—Plato was attempting to present the views and character of the historical Socrates.

These pieces follow a chronological sequence, spanning the few weeks before and after Socrates' trial and conviction for impiety. In the *Euthyphro*, Socrates is waiting to attend a preliminary hearing before the city's magistrates when he strikes up a conversation with another legal petitioner, Euthyphro. In the *Apology*[1] we hear Socrates' unsuccessful defense in response to the indictment against him. The *Crito* takes place in Socrates' prison cell, where he is waiting to be executed, and deals with Socrates' reasons for refusing to accept the help of his wealthy friend Crito and escape from Athens. Finally, the concluding section of the *Phaedo* included here describes Socrates' demeanor and conversation at the time of his death.

These dialogues are instances of a fourth-century BCE literary genre called "Socratic conversations" (*Sokratikoi logoi*) in which people who knew Socrates wrote imagined reconstructions of his conversations. Dialogues by Plato and the historian Xenophon (c. 430–354 BCE) are the only examples of this genre that survived, but others were written by many of his contemporaries.

Plato attended Socrates' trial and, although the *Apology* is certainly not a verbatim account of what Socrates actually said, it is likely that it does not depart too far from the flavor and spirit of Socrates' words (since Plato's dialogue would have been read by many people who were actually there). Plato was not personally present at Socrates' death, but he knew people who were. The *Euthyphro* and the *Crito*, by contrast, although they involve real people, were not literal records of actual conversations or events—and would not have been expected to be so by Plato's readers—but rather exemplify the thoughts, manners, and personality of Socrates, and in so doing they use Socrates to explore Plato's own ideas.

---

1   *Apology* is the traditional name for this dialogue, but it might be better named *Socrates' Defense*—the standard name comes from the Greek *apologia*, which means defense.

Some Useful Background Information

The Political Context

In ancient Greece, the city (*polis*) was the primary political unit—approximately equivalent to states today. Although the Greeks at the time did think of themselves as members of a common people, their main allegiance was to their home *polis*, and cities differed widely in their culture and forms of government. Socrates and Plato lived during a period of major transition for their home state of Athens. Athens was the most powerful and culturally influential Greek city-state in the Athenian "Golden Age" of the 440s and 430s BCE, but 431 saw the beginning of brutal wars for dominance between Athens and the competing city-state of Sparta, ending with the humiliating defeat of Athens in 404. This was followed by yet another turn of fortune: the decline of Sparta and partial re-establishment of Athenian fortunes in the 370s.

The crucial political event that forms the background for Socrates' trial and execution was the final defeat of Athens in the long Peloponnesian War against Sparta, which happened in 404 BCE, five years before Socrates' trial. This, obviously, was a crushing blow for Athenian self-confidence and brought about a crescendo in the already ongoing search for someone to blame for the city's misfortunes. The democratic government and its generals naturally shouldered a large part of this guilt, and so this government was toppled and replaced by a puppet junta of Athenian aristocrats supported and controlled by the Spartan army: these were known as the Thirty Tyrants. The Tyrants sought to secure their political position with a bloody campaign of repression, but this had the effect of sparking a civil war in Athens in which, the following year, the forces of the democrats were victorious. This new government tried to bring order back to the Athenian state by forming an alliance with moderate members of the anti-democratic, oligarchical faction and proclaiming a blanket amnesty for crimes committed during the previous few years, including under the rule of the Thirty.

In general, Socrates was overtly apolitical throughout his life, refusing to take sides with the various factions that fought over control of Athens, but he was also adamant in refusing to participate in anything that he considered to be unjust or illegal, even when such refusals endangered his own safety. (He describes some of these episodes in his speech in the *Apology*.) In both these ways he was unusual for his time, and—perhaps ironically—both were causes for public suspicion of him.

Furthermore, despite his intention to steer clear of politics, he nevertheless was associated with several figures who were perceived to be enemies of democracy in Athens, three powerful men in particular. Alcibiades—a close friend of Socrates who often boasted of his association with him—was a rich, charming, arrogant man who had led Athens to crushing military disaster, blasphemed against one of the most important Athenian religious cults, the Eleusinian Mysteries, and then turned traitor and fled to the Spartans and helped them attack his former home city. Critias, Socrates' student and a first cousin of his mother, was the aristocratic leader of the Thirty Tyrants who controlled Athens after its defeat by Sparta and the suspension of democracy, and another one of the tyrants, Charmides, was also Socrates' pupil (and Plato's uncle).

Socrates publicly denounced the illegal actions of the Thirty Tyrants (not because they were undemocratic, but because they were unconstitutional and unjust), and refused Critias's demand that he stop associating with and influencing the young men of the city. Instead of executing him, however, Critias sought to implicate him in the short-lived oligarchy by commanding him to arrest a wealthy enemy of the regime, Leon of Salamis, seize his property, and execute him; as recounted in the *Apology*, Socrates refused to participate, but Leon was nevertheless killed.

During the rule of the Thirty Tyrants some 1,500 Athenians were murdered by the regime. None of the main culprits were available to be officially tried for their crimes, because of the general amnesty or because they had already died or escaped the city—though in one way or another almost all of them met untimely ends—and so it is quite possible that one of the undercurrents in Socrates' trial was that he was being made a scapegoat for the recent horrors.

The Religious Context

Ancient Greek religious beliefs form an important background to the Platonic dialogues collected here. Greek religion was polytheistic,[1] and different cities and regions worshipped somewhat different collections of deities. The gods mentioned in these dialogues include Zeus, god of the sky and leader of the gods; Hera, goddess of women and Zeus's wife (and sister); Athena, goddess of wisdom and craft; Hephaistos (sometimes spelled Hephaestus), god of blacksmiths and fire; and Asclepius, the god of healing. The city of Athens bears the

---

1   Although Socrates and Plato were both attracted to, and perhaps persuaded by, the idea of monotheism.

same name as Athena, who was considered the divine patroness of the city, and the Parthenon—named for Athena Parthenos or the virgin Athena—was a major temple and center of worship for her. Hephaistos was also a particularly important god for Athens, because the city was a center of manufacturing and craftsmanship. Finally, a principal god who is mentioned obliquely is Apollo, god of poetry and prophecy, among other things; it is Apollo to whom the oracle at Delphi is sacred, and thus he is the god who gave Socrates his divine mission (and may be the god who speaks to him through his "divine sign").

In addition to the gods, the Greeks believed in a number of demigods: half-god, half-mortal children of liaisons between gods and mortals. Of these, Heracles and Tantalos are both mentioned in the dialogues. Heracles (known to the Romans as Hercules) was a son of Zeus and the ideal hero to the Greeks, a semi-divine figure who used both his strength and his intelligence to fight against various monsters on behalf of humanity. Tantalos (or Tantalus) was another son of Zeus, but instead of being a hero he murdered his son and tried to feed him to the gods as an offering. For this he was punished by being placed in the deepest part of the Underworld, where he was constantly offered food and drink, which then receded just outside his grasp when he tried to take them.[1] The text mentions "the money of Tantalos"; he was a king who derived great wealth from mines he controlled, and also his association with the Underworld in Greek myth would have had overtones for Plato's contemporaries, who saw the realms below ground as a source of mineral riches.

Finally, the ancient Greeks believed in beings even older than the gods of Olympus, two of whom are mentioned in these dialogues: the giant Titans including Cronos, father of Zeus; and Cronos's own father Ouranos (sometimes spelled Uranus), who was the elemental Greek god personifying the sky.

Life in Plato's Athens, and in classical Greece generally, was thoroughly permeated by religion. The year was shaped by a succession of regular religious festivals, and everything—from politics to warfare to crafts to agriculture to the arts—had a religious character. Of particular importance was the role of religion in contributing to the solidarity of the community, and religious observance was a public act often enforced by civic laws. Ritual sacrifice of animals such as oxen, sheep, and pigs was a central, and frequent, feature of Greek religious life and served to reinforce the proper relationship not only between humans and gods but also between members of the community. Social groups—families, demes (local regions), clubs, cities, and even the

---

1   This is the origin of the verb *to tantalize*.

wider Greek nation—were defined as those who worshipped the same gods.[1]

Since religious ritual was what kept the gods' good will and support of one's community alive, impiety was a serious crime: piety was a form of patriotism, which, it was believed, had serious real-world consequences if it was neglected. There was no separation between the modern concepts of "church" and "state" in ancient Greece, and so religious authority was inseparable from secular power. Major sacred rites were performed by magistrates or prominent citizens on behalf of the city. Individual gods had their priests, but these were typically part-time holy men with secular "day jobs," and there were no institutions to train and certify priests or to ensure any kind of doctrinal orthodoxy.

The closest things to religious professionals in classical Greece were seers and oracles. A seer was someone who interpreted dreams or various patterns in nature, such as the flight of birds or the entrails of a sacrificed animal, in order to answer questions put to the gods. Seers—such as Euthyphro—were consulted often, including before public activities such as military campaigns or political decisions; they were frequently influential members of the social elite and were taken extremely seriously, although decision-making power remained with the generals or citizen assembly.

Oracles were specific sacred locations at which, at particular times, the gods spoke directly to people, together with the priestesses and priests who interpreted these pronouncements. In the *Apology* Socrates mentions the oracle at Delphi (about 100 km northwest of Athens), which was the most important oracle in ancient Greece and thought to stand at the center of the world; it was generally considered to be infallible, so Socrates' allusion to it has great weight. When Socrates asserts that he has a mission from god to examine and improve the people of Athens, he is being perfectly sincere and literal.

An example of the tight integration of religion into civic life, and of its life-and-death importance, is the episode of the mutilations of the herms (*hermai*), statues of the face and phallus of the god Hermes that served as sacred boundary markers surrounding the city. In 415, in the depths of the Peloponnesian War, Athens was mounting an invasion of Sicily. On the eve of the departure of the fleet, the shocking discovery was made that almost all of the herms had been vandalized overnight. The city was appalled by this act of sacrilege and also feared

---

1   The period of upheaval in Athens caused by the disruptions of the Peloponnesian War and the defeat at the hands of Sparta and its allies led to a flowering of new cults and religious rites in Athens. For example, the worship of Asclepius—mentioned in the *Phaedo*—was a new import to Athens during the war.

a conspiracy against the democracy, and a commission was swiftly established to investigate not only who had defaced the herms, but also any crimes of irreverence toward the city's gods. Rewards were offered for those who informed on their neighbors, and the following few months saw a spreading moral panic in which hundreds of people were tortured, imprisoned, exiled, and executed for the crime of impiety. Among those who were accused were many of Socrates' close friends and students, such as Alcibiades, Phaedrus, Charmides, and Critias. In the end, it turned out that the actual culprits in the mutilations of the herms had been the members of a young men's drinking club, one of whom confessed, and that many of the accusations of impiety had been trumped up by lying informants. But by then, of course, the damage had been done.

One final point regarding the religious context of these dialogues: the notion of the soul, as Plato understands it, is not precisely the same as the modern notion (although Platonic doctrines of the soul were important precursors to the Christian concept). According to Plato, the soul, or *psyche*, is the thing that brings life to the body; it is the "shade" that persists after the death of the body; and it is essentially rational. However, it is not a kind of non-physical substance; instead, it is more analogous to a really existing but abstract object such as the Form of the Good. The Greeks had no clear theory of an afterlife and paid no special attention to life after death; their religious hopes were generally focussed on success in this life.

The Legal Context

Athenian law, unlike modern legal systems, made no distinction between private and public interests: private individuals were entitled to prosecute people, not because they had been personally wronged, but on behalf of the public interest. It was not unusual for citizens to consider it their moral duty to prosecute other individuals for harming the city, and this is what happened to Socrates.

In the Athenian legal system there was no equivalent of an attorney general—no one to either permit or to disallow a legal process. And during the trial there was no presiding judge able to make decisions about the adequacy or relevance of the evidence being presented. There was also no judge to decide on a penalty for plaintiffs found guilty: in cases like Socrates', the prosecutor would argue for a penalty, the accused would make a counter-argument for a different penalty, and the jury would vote to decide between the two.

The charge of impiety—of not showing proper respect to the city's gods—was not an unusual one. Some of the most famous citizens of

Athens had to respond to similar legal accusations, including the sculptor and architect Phidias, the playwrights and poets Sophocles and Euripides, and the philosophers Anaxagoras, Aristotle, and Theophrastus. (On the other hand, the charge of corrupting the youth does seem to be unusual, and it may have been formulated specifically for Socrates.)

To us all of this may seem flawed and unsatisfactory, but to Socrates (and Plato) his trial was a perfectly normal and acceptable instance of Athenian law and democracy in action.

The trial took place in a large building—basically just an open space with walls and seating—in the marketplace at the corner of the Acropolis. It lasted no more than a single day. Present were the 500 (or possibly 501) jury members, chosen by lottery, plus a crowd of curious onlookers, as even at the time the trial was attracting a great deal of attention. A substantial proportion of the jury and audience would have known Socrates personally and many more would have heard of him—Athens at the time had a population of about 150,000 people, about the size of Alexandria, Virginia, or Guelph, Ontario, or Oxford, England; of these, perhaps 20,000 would have been eligible for jury duty.

Imprisonment was not a normal punishment in ancient Greece—standard punishments were fines, loss of citizenship, exile, or death—and so it was unusual to keep prisoners more than a day or two before their execution or while they arranged payment of their fine. Socrates' imprisonment was extended to some thirty days, since no execution was permitted during the sacred festival of Apollo and the end of the festival, marked by the return of a special boat from the holy island of Delos, was delayed by contrary winds keeping the boat at sea. Socrates, then, had ample opportunity to escape from his prison, which he could have done by simply digging through its earthen wall or through bribery. But he chose not to.

Sophism

Another factor in the trial of Socrates was the (false) popular association of Socrates with the school of Sophism. Sophists were traveling teachers who, for payment, would teach young male citizens the art of rhetoric, or persuasive public speaking. This was a skill of great practical importance since legal and political decisions were made by assemblies of citizens and were based on the persuasiveness of the involved parties. Because their teaching was in great demand, Sophists were often popular, courted by the powerful, and became very wealthy from the fees their students paid.

On the other hand, they were not to be trusted and their teachings were often thought to have a corrosive effect on democracy and good governance because they explicitly taught the art of making the weaker of two arguments appear to be the stronger. That is, they were not concerned with rationality or good judgement but simply with persuasion, and they prided themselves on their ability to make true claims seem false. In this way, they were a clear and present danger to conventional or traditional belief. Gorgias, for example, a prominent Sophist, advertised himself as being able to make even paradoxical, absurd positions appear reasonable; and he taught a particular, theatrical style of speaking that was intended, literally, to cast a kind of spell on the audience that acted like a drug to make them more suggestible.

How Important and Influential Are These Dialogues?

It is difficult to overestimate the influence of Plato's thought on the history of philosophy. The dialogues collected here contain seminal early explorations of several big ideas: the relationship between religion and morality (and whether it is coherent to suppose that morality is grounded in religious belief); the nature of death, and whether or not it is a harm; the health of the immortal soul; the nature of goodness, and of the good life; and the question of what we owe to the state and its laws, including a very influential expression of the notion that there is some sort of implicit contract between the state and its citizens that is the grounding for our obligation to obey the law.

Furthermore, these short dialogues provide a powerful introduction to what philosophy *is*: the examination of every preconception, no matter how conventional or comfortable, and following the arguments wherever they may lead, in service of the overriding goal of uncovering the truth.

A second way in which these dialogues are important is as the main source for the inspirational example of Socrates. Over the centuries his "martyrdom" at the hands of his fellow citizens has been held up as an iconic moral example, perhaps second in the Western tradition only to Jesus, with whom he is often compared, for Socrates' unwavering commitment to his own moral principles and his steadfastness in the face of death.

Cast of Characters

All the characters that appear in these dialogues were real people. Here is an overview of some of the main characters:

Euthyphro: A seer or prophet; that is, someone who was a professional interpreter of the wishes of the gods. Little is known about him beyond what is revealed in Plato's dialogues.

Anytus: One of Socrates' prosecutors. A wealthy democrat, he had been a not-very-successful general during the wars with Sparta who had escaped punishment for his failures by bribing the courts. He hated the Sophists and, probably influenced by Aristophanes' play *Clouds* (originally produced in 423 BCE), associated Socrates with them.

Meletus: The main presenter of the case against Socrates. He was a fairly young man and a religious zealot who had previously been involved in bringing legal charges of impiety.

Lycon: Little is known about Lycon, Socrates' third accuser, although he is referred to as "an orator," perhaps implying a politician who uses his skill with rhetoric to influence the democratic masses in order to gain power and fame for himself. If so, Socrates and he would have been natural enemies.

Gorgias: Nicknamed "the nihilist," Gorgias was a prominent Sophist from Sicily who settled in Athens as an old man and became extremely popular and in great demand as a teacher of wealthy young men. When he died he was rich enough to commission a gold statue of himself for a public temple.

Chaerephon: A charismatic, impetuous, popular "man about town," Chaerephon is mentioned (unflatteringly) in no fewer than three of Aristophanes' comedies. Both Aristophanes and Xenophon describe him as one of Socrates' closest companions, and he appears in three Platonic dialogues.

Anaxagoras of Clazomenae: A precursor of Socrates (he died in about 428 BCE), Anaxagoras was born in the area that is modern-day Turkey and is sometimes credited with being the first person to bring philosophy to Athens. He developed a sophisticated cosmology—which in some ways was the distant ancestor of modern atomic theory—and for his pains he was tried for impiety and forced into exile.

Crito: By the end of Socrates' life, Crito was his most loyal and closest friend. He was about Socrates' age and grew up with him in the same deme. However, he is portrayed in contemporary accounts as being more pragmatically than philosophically inclined.

Critoboulus: Crito's eldest son and, like his father, a wealthy farmer rather than a philosopher.

Apollodorus of Phaleron: A volatile, aggressively loyal, and wealthy man who was another prominent student of Socrates. He is not portrayed as an independent thinker but as someone who uncritically and fervently accepted Socrates' views.

Simmias of Thebes: A disciple of Socrates but also a philosopher in his own right who wrote a score of dialogues, none of which have survived.

Cebes of Thebes: A friend of Simmias, and like him a philosophical follower of Socrates.

Phaedo of Elis: A philosopher who was captured in war as a young man and held as a slave by a wealthy Athenian until he was freed by Socrates (or rather by a rich friend of Socrates—perhaps Crito—at his request), and who took Socrates as his mentor.

Echecrates of Phlius: A Pythagorean philosopher who held Socrates in high regard, and the person to whom Phaedo is depicted as describing Socrates' final hours.

Timeline

c. 470	Birth of Socrates.
478	Defeat of the Persian invasion of Greece by a coalition led by Athens (the Delian League), and the start of the Athenian "Golden Age."
454	The Delian League becomes, in effect, the Athenian empire, as Athens takes control of its finances and military.
445	Pericles is elected main democratic leader and general of the army, a position he holds until his death by being repeatedly re-elected.
c. 437	Anaxagoras is banished from Athens after being tried for impiety.
431	Start of the Peloponnesian War between the Athenian empire (a mainly naval power) and Sparta and its (mostly land-based) allies.
430	Outbreak of plague (typhoid fever) in Athens.
429	Death of Pericles from plague.
c. 427	Birth of Plato.
423	Public performance of Aristophanes' play *Clouds*, mocking Socrates and probably making him notorious in the city.
c. 416	Socrates marries Xanthippe.

415	There is a rash of trials and executions for impiety, including of many of Socrates' associates, following the mutilations of the *hermai*, the symbolic Athenian border markers.
413	Another play by Aristophanes, *Birds*, is performed, which also includes an attack on Socrates.
412	Athenian morale is at a low point, following revolts by several of its subject-allies.
411	An Athenian coup briefly overthrows democracy and replaces it with oligarchy: the rule of the Four Hundred.
406	Athens wins a sea battle (the battle of Arginusae), but at such a major cost that the city's military power is effectively destroyed. Socrates is an overseer of the Athenian citizens' council (the *boule*) at this time and refuses to allow the responsible generals to be illegally prosecuted. After his term ends, the generals are prosecuted anyway and executed.
404	Athens is finally defeated; this is followed by a reaction against its democratic leaders, who were blamed for the defeat, and the rule of the Thirty Tyrants (backed by the Spartan army).
403	Restoration of Athenian democracy after a brief civil war.
399	Trial and execution of Socrates.
399–387	Plato writes *Euthyphro, Apology, Crito*.
395	Start of the Corinthian War, sparked by Spartan imperialism.
387	Plato's first visit to Sicily.
387–367	Plato writes *Phaedo*.
c. 385	Plato founds the Academy.
384	Birth of Aristotle.
371	Defeat of Sparta and establishment of the second Athenian League.
c. 367	Aristotle joins the Academy. Plato's second visit to Sicily.
360	Plato escapes Sicily.
c. 347	Death of Plato.
338	Athens is defeated by Macedonia, and soon after ceases to be an independent power.

Suggestions for Critical Reflection

1. Socrates often speaks ironically. For example, at the start of the *Euthyphro* he begins by praising Meletus for his wisdom in bringing the indictment against him, and he reacts similarly to Euthyphro when he learns that he is bringing charges against his own father. What do you think is the purpose of this ironical tone?

2. In the *Euthyphro* Socrates famously asks whether right action (piety) is loved by the gods because it is right, or if an action is right simply because it is approved of by the gods (10a). What is the difference between the two options? Socrates does not seem to take the second option seriously, instead focusing on the first; why do you think this might be?

3. Socrates claims that "the beloved is not pious, Euthyphro, nor is the pious beloved by the gods, as you claim, but the one is different from the other" (10e). How does he reach this conclusion?

4. How does Socrates defend himself in the *Apology*? Why does he not argue directly that he and his followers were models of civic virtue and respectful of the traditional gods?

5. Socrates is depicted, in the *Apology*, as going to some lengths to differentiate himself from the Sophists. Why do you think he does this?

6. Socrates says, in the *Apology*, "either I do not corrupt, or if I do corrupt, I do so unintentionally" (26a). What is his argument for this claim, and how persuasive is it?

7. When Socrates, perhaps unwisely, says, "Rest assured that if you kill me for being the kind of person I describe, you will not harm me more than yourselves" (30c), what do you think he means?

8. In the final section of the *Apology*, Socrates argues that death may well be a good thing. What are his arguments for this? What do you think of them?

9. In the *Crito*, Socrates represents the city of Athens as saying to its citizens, "whoever remains with us, having observed how we decide lawsuits and take care of other civic matters, we claim that this man by his action has now made an agreement with us to do what we command him to do" (51e). How does Socrates argue that the city may be right to say this? If true, what are the implications of this claim?

10. Socrates argues in the *Crito* that, since he could not persuade the citizens of Athens to spare him, he must accept their judgement and agree to die. Yet he also argues passionately, especially in the *Apology*, that he cannot accept that any human

being has the right to prevent him from doing his god-given duty of philosophizing and teaching others to philosophize: that is, he argues that there are limits to what a law can impose on its citizens. There seems to be a tension between these two positions. What do you think? Is Socrates really contradicting himself?

11. Socrates' last words are said to be reminding Crito to make a sacrifice to Asclepius, the god of healing (118a). What do you think might be the significance of this?

12. Socrates holds that wisdom contributes to genuine self-interest: that doing the right thing is always in one's own best interests. Yet, in the end, he is executed for his behavior and because he has refused to do the things that might have saved him (such as giving up doing philosophy, or accepting Crito's help to flee from Athens). What are we to make of this?

Suggestions for Further Reading

Part of the fun of grappling with these dialogues is learning about the very different, and fascinating, way of life of ancient Athens. A couple of interesting and accessible resources for this include Robert Parker, "Greek Religion," in *The Oxford History of the Classical World*, ed. John Boardman, Jasper Griffin, and Oswyn Murray (Oxford University Press, 1986), and K.J. Dover's *Greek Popular Morality in the Time of Plato and Aristotle* (Basil Blackwell, 1974, reprinted by Hackett in 1994). The British Joint Association of Classical Teachers has produced a reliable, readable (illustrated) book called *The World of Athens: An Introduction to Classical Athenian Culture* (Cambridge University Press, 2008). Another interesting read is *The Mutilation of the Herms: Unpacking an Ancient Mystery*, self-published by Debra Hamel in 2012 (http://www.dhamel.com/the-mutilation-of-the-herms).

Some more context comes from *Xenophon, Conversations of Socrates*, translated by Hugh Tredennick and revised by Robin Waterfield (Penguin, 1990), and an enjoyable modern translation of Aristophanes' *Clouds* is by Peter Meineck (Hackett, 1998).

Probably the best short introduction to the philosophical context in which Plato was writing is still Terence Irwin's superb *Classical Thought* (Oxford University Press, 1989). Paul Johnson, *Socrates: A Man for Our Times* (Penguin, 2011) vividly describes the "celebrity culture" of ancient Athens, while Robin Waterfield, *Why Socrates Died: Dispelling the Myths* (Faber and Faber, 2009) is, as well as being an outstanding account of the context of Socrates' trial, particularly interesting as a defense of Socrates' accusers, or at least an attempt to explain their actions as being rational and understandable. (As Waterfield puts it, "Socrates would have been the last to want to leave a cultural icon unexamined.") Also well worth consulting are C.C.W. Taylor, *Socrates: A Very Short Introduction* (Oxford University Press, 1998); *A Companion to Socrates*, edited by Sara Ahbel-Rappe and Rachana Kamtekar (Blackwell, 2006); T.C. Brickhouse and N.D. Smith, *The Routledge Philosophy Guidebook to Plato and the Trial of Socrates* (Routledge, 2004); and James A. Colaiaco, *Socrates Against Athens* (Routledge, 2001).

There is a *Cambridge Companion to Socrates*, ed. Donald R. Morrison (Cambridge University Press, 2010); *The Cambridge Companion to Plato*, ed. Richard Kraut (Cambridge University Press, 1992), is also of interest, especially the chapters by Terry Penner on "Socrates and the Early Dialogues" and by Michael L. Morgan on "Plato and Greek Religion." Finally, two more scholarly works of very high quality are Gregory Vlastos, *Socrates: Ironist and Moral Philosopher* (Cambridge University Press, 1991), and T.C. Brickhouse and N.D. Smith, *Socrates on Trial* (Oxford University Press, 1989).

Translators' Note

The current translation aims foremost at accuracy and completeness, including the liveliness of the dialogue form. We have striven to preserve the natural flow of the speech. This both helps and, in a way, hurts the readability of the translation. After all, these texts portray people speaking, and speaking to one another, and humans are not always the most eloquent of speakers. This is recreated by Plato. The *Apology* is almost entirely composed of Socrates speaking at length to his judges and so he sometimes finds himself, because he goes on for quite a while, and keeps inserting qualifications, and then loses his way, moving to a new grammatical construction. Similarly, characters sometimes pile one clause on top of another. Usually these run-on sentences are easy to follow and the effect is often an increasing intensity, but once or twice in *Apology* Socrates seems rather to be trying to find his way into an idea and is less than eloquent as a result. Whether the character is in control or in difficulties, we have attempted to preserve his pattern of speech. The general upshot of these considerations is that these translations are best read at speaking speed.

The translations were made from the 1995 Oxford Classical Text of Duke et al. (However, we prefer ἐρῶντα τῷ ἐρωμένῳ at *Euthyphro* 14b4, retain οὐ at *Apology* 27e7, and give ἀληθῆ λέγεις to Crito at *Crito* 48b1.)

The commentaries of Adam (*Euthyphro*, *Apology*, *Crito*) and Burnet (in *Plato: Euthyphro, Apology of Socrates, Crito*) proved invaluable throughout. In addition, for *Euthyphro*, some useful suggestions were found in the editions by Graves, Heidel, and Wells; for *Apology*, Flagg, and Helm's *Plato: Apology*; for *Crito*, Cron/Dyer, Flagg, Tyler, and Wagner; and for *Phaedo*, Stanford.

We express our gratitude to Virginia Wesleyan College for supporting both translators during the original preparation of these translations in 2007, from the Faculty Summer Development Fund (Woods) and from the Undergraduate Research Fund (Pack).

We would also like to thank Dustin Platter and Seosamh MacCoille, and Laura Buzzard and Stephen Latta at Broadview Press, for commenting on drafts of the translations.

Readers are encouraged to send corrections to the translations. This is best done by e-mail, to cathalwoods@gmail.com.

Cathal Woods
Ryan Pack

Euthyphro

Introduction

In this dialogue, which takes place a few weeks before Socrates' trial, Socrates is on his way to "the porch of the king"—that is, the open building or walkway in the Agora that was the meeting place for the King Archon, who despite his archaic title was of one of nine elected officials in Athens with mostly formal functions. Socrates had to attend on the "king" in order to hear the charges being brought against him by Meletus, and to have the date set for his trial.

On his way he bumps into a professional religious prophet, or soothsayer, named Euthyphro, who is also there to meet with the King Archon—though in Euthyphro's case it is to bring an indictment rather than to receive one. As is Socrates' habit, he falls into conversation with Euthyphro and is soon quizzing him about whether he has really thought through the justification for his actions.

The main subject of the *Euthyphro* is a particular moral virtue— that of piety or holiness, which is to say showing proper respect for religion and the gods (literally, knowledge of how to properly perform ritual prayers and sacrifices). However, the notion is somewhat broader than it might initially seem: insofar as the gods approve generally of morally good behavior, to show proper respect for the gods will involve behaving well more generally.

Socrates fairly quickly turns the discussion to an attempt to find the essence or definition of piety—the fundamental thing that all pious actions have in common. (The particular murder that Euthyphro is prosecuting is merely an example of something that might be an impious action, and not the central topic of the dialogue.) Euthyphro's first attempt to answer this question is to say that "what is beloved by the gods is pious, and what is not beloved by them is impious," but Socrates shows him that this is inadequate as a definition. He argues against it in two ways, but it is the second that really counts; this more fundamental objection to the definition emerges when Socrates asks, "Is the pious loved by the gods because it's pious, or it is pious because it is loved?"

The final stage of the dialogue deals with piety as a particular type of right action ("the pious is a part of the just")—pious actions are those that constitute appropriate interaction with the gods. Euthyphro is confident that he is on solid ground here, as an expert on dealing with the gods, but Socrates once again ties him into logical knots and shows that merely identifying what the gods like is not yet to show what about it *makes* it worth liking. (Analogously, your favorite music is not *made into* good music by the mere fact you like it—there must be something about it that is already good, and it is for this reason that you like it.)

At this point Euthyphro suddenly remembers that he has urgent business elsewhere, and to Socrates' disappointment the conversation comes to an abrupt end.

Euthyphro

2a   Euthyphro: What new thing has happened, Socrates, that you have abandoned your stomping grounds in the Lyceum[1] and are now spending your time here, around the porch of the king[2]? For surely you too are not involved in some suit before the king,[3] as I am.

Socrates: No, Euthyphro, the Athenians don't just call it a suit, but a public indictment.[4]

b   Euthyphro: What do you mean? Someone has indicted you, I suppose, since I certainly wouldn't accuse you of the opposite, you indicting someone else.

Socrates: Certainly not.

Euthyphro: So someone else is indicting you?

---

1   *Lyceum* A gymnasium outside the walls of Athens.
2   *the porch of the king* The "porch" is a covered walkway in the Athenian *agora* (marketplace or forum).
3   *before the king* The "king" was one of nine *archons* or magistrates. At this stage of the proceedings, accusations would be lodged and testimony recorded from those involved and from witnesses. The King Archon was in charge of religious matters. Socrates is there because he has been charged with a religious crime (not acknowledging the gods of the city); Euthyphro is there because he believes that his father, as a murderer, is polluting the religious spaces of the city, which therefore need to be purified. (See section 57 of Aristotle's *Athenian Constitution*.)
4   *a public indictment* It was up to individuals (in Socrates' case, Meletus, along with Anytus and Lycon) to bring cases on behalf of the city.

Socrates: Absolutely.

Euthyphro: Who is this person?

Socrates: I don't know the man very well myself, Euthyphro; I think he is a young and unknown person. Anyway, I believe they call him Meletus. He is from the Pitthean deme,[1] if you know of a Meletus from Pitthos with straight hair, not much of a beard, and with a slightly hooked nose.

Euthyphro: I don't know him, Socrates. But what charge has he indicted you on?　　　　c

Socrates: On what charge? A not undistinguished one, I think, as it's no small thing for a young man to be knowledgeable about so important an issue. For he, he says, knows how the young are corrupted and who their corruptors are. He's probably somebody wise, and having seen how I in my ignorance corrupt the people of his generation, he is coming to tattle on me to the city, as though it were his mother. And he alone seems to me to be starting out in politics correctly, because the correct way is to first give one's attention to how our young people will be the best possible, just as a good farmer probably cares first for his young plants, and after this for the others as well. And so Meletus too is presumably first weeding out those of us who corrupt the 　3a sprouting young people, as he puts it. Then after this it's clear that, having turned his attention to the older people, he will become a source of many great goods for the city—this is likely to happen to him, having started off in this way.

Euthyphro: I wish it were so, Socrates, but I'm terrified that the opposite might happen. Because it seems to me that by trying to wrong you he is starting out by recklessly harming the hearth of the city. Do tell me, just what does he say you're doing to corrupt the young?

Socrates: Extraordinary things, you remarkable man, at least to hear 　b him describe them. For he says I am a maker of gods, and because I make novel gods and do not acknowledge the old ones, he indicts me for their sake, he says.

1　*deme* An administrative division of Attica, the broader region in which Athens is located.

Euthyphro: I understand, Socrates. It's because of the divine sign[1] that you say comes to you occasionally. And so he has lodged this indictment on the grounds that you are an innovator concerning religious ideas and he is surely coming to the court intending to slander you, knowing that such things are easily misrepresented to the many. Indeed in my case too, whenever I say something in the assembly about religious matters, foretelling the future for them, they ridicule me as a madman, even though nothing in my foretelling was untrue. Even so, they envy all of us who are like this. We should think nothing of them but fight them on their own ground.

Socrates: But my dear Euthyphro, being ridiculed is probably no big deal; indeed it seems to me that it doesn't matter much to the Athenians if they think someone is clever, provided that he is not capable of teaching his wisdom. They become outraged, though, with anyone they suspect of also trying to shape others in some way, whether because they are envious, as you claim, or for some other reason.

Euthyphro: Which is why I have no great desire to have it put to the test, how they feel about me.

Socrates: It's perhaps because you seem to rarely make yourself available and appear unwilling to teach your wisdom, whereas I fear that, because of my love of people, I strike them as someone who is bursting to talk to everybody, and not just without demanding payment, but would even be glad to compensate anyone who was willing to listen to me. So as I was saying, if they intend to laugh at me, as you said happens to you, there would be nothing unpleasant about spending time in court playing around and laughing. But if they are going to be serious, in that case it's unclear how things will turn out, except to you prophets.

Euthyphro: Well, it will probably be nothing, Socrates, and you will fight your case satisfactorily, as I think I will fight mine, too.

Socrates: Yes, what exactly is your suit, Euthyphro? Are you defending or prosecuting it?

Euthyphro: I am prosecuting.

Socrates: Whom?

---

1   *divine sign* See *Apology* 31b and 41a–c.

Euthyphro: A man whom by pursuing I will again appear mad.   4a

Socrates: But why? You're pursuing someone who flies?

Euthyphro: He is a long way from flying; indeed he happens to be well advanced in years.

Socrates: Who is he?

Euthyphro: My own father.

Socrates: Your father, you fantastic fellow?!

Euthyphro: Absolutely.

Socrates: But what is the charge, and what are the circumstances?

Euthyphro: Murder, Socrates.

Socrates: Heracles! Surely most people don't know what is correct in such a situation, since I don't think that just anyone could take care of this correctly, but only someone, I suspect, who has progressed a long   b
way in wisdom.

Euthyphro: By Zeus, a long way indeed, Socrates.

Socrates: Surely the person killed by your father is one of your relatives? It must be, since you would not prosecute him for murder on behalf of a stranger?

Euthyphro: It's ridiculous, Socrates, that you think it makes a difference whether the man killed is a stranger or a relative, rather than that it is necessary to attend only to this: whether the killer killed legally or not—and if it was legal, to let him go, and if not, to prosecute him, even if the killer shares your hearth and eats at the same table. Be-   c
cause the pollution is the same, if you knowingly associate with such a man and do not purify both yourself and him by prosecuting him in law.

The victim, as a matter of fact, was one of my hired men, and when we were farming in Naxos[1] he was working for us there. Well, he got drunk, became angry with another one of our household

---

1   *Naxos* A Greek island that was an Athenian colony.

slaves, and slit the man's throat. So my father bound his feet and hands, threw him into some ditch, and sent a man here to inquire of the interpreter of religious law about what should be done. But during that time he paid no attention to the bound man and neglected him, thinking him a murderer and that it would be no big thing if he died as well, which then in fact happened, as he died of hunger and cold and of his bonds before the messenger returned from the interpreter.

d

That's why both my father and my other relatives are angry, because I am prosecuting my father on behalf of a murderer, when he didn't kill him, they say, or if he did in fact kill him, well, since the man he killed was a murderer, one should not be concerned about such people—because it's unholy for a son to prosecute his father for murder, they say, not really knowing, Socrates, how the religious law stands with respect to holiness and unholiness.

e

Socrates: But before Zeus, Euthyphro, do you think you have such accurate knowledge about how the religious laws stand, about both piety and impiety, that, with these things having taken place in the way you describe, you are not afraid that by prosecuting your father you in turn might be committing an impiety?

5a   Euthyphro: I would be of no use, Socrates, and neither would Euthyphro be better than the majority of men, if I did not have accurate knowledge of all such matters.

Socrates: In that case it would be excellent for me to become a student of yours, marvelous Euthyphro, and prior to this dispute with Meletus I will challenge him exactly as follows, saying that while even in the past I used to make knowing the religious law my top priority, now, because he says I err by judging rashly and innovating with respect to the religious laws, I have even become your student.

b

And I could say, "If you agree, Meletus, that Euthyphro is wise in such matters, then believe that I worship properly, too, and do not charge me. If not, see about bringing a charge against him, my teacher, rather than me, since he corrupts the elderly—me and his father—by teaching me and by rebuking and chastising him." And if I don't convince him and he doesn't withdraw the charge or indict *you* in my place, shouldn't I say in court the exact same thing as I said when challenging him?

c   Euthyphro: Yes, by Zeus, Socrates. If he tried to indict me I think I would uncover in what way he is unsound and we would find that the discussion in court would be about him, long before it was about me.

Socrates: And indeed, my dear Euthyphro, I recognize this and want to become a student of yours, seeing how practically everyone else and Meletus himself pretends not to notice you, but he sees through me so clearly and easily that he indicts me for impiety. So now, by Zeus, explain to me what you were just now claiming to know clearly: what sort of thing do you say holiness is, and unholiness, with respect to murder and everything else as well? Or isn't the pious the same as itself in every action,[1] and the impious in turn is the complete opposite of the pious but the same as itself, and everything that in fact turns out to be impious has a single form with respect to its impiousness?

d

Euthyphro: It certainly is, Socrates.

Socrates: So tell me, what do you say the pious is, and what is the impious?

Euthyphro: Well then, I claim that the pious is what I am doing now, prosecuting someone who is guilty of wrongdoing—either of murder or temple robbery or anything else of the sort, whether it happens to be one's father or mother or whoever else—and the impious is failing to prosecute. For observe, Socrates, how great a proof I will give you that this is how the law stands, one I have already given to others as well, which shows such actions to be correct—not yielding to impious people, that is, no matter who they happen to be. Because these very people also happen to worship Zeus as the best and most just of the gods, and agree that he put his own father in bonds because he unjustly swallowed his sons, and the father too castrated his own father for other similar reasons.[2] Yet they are sore at me because I am prosecuting my father for his injustice. And so they say contradictory things about the gods and about me.

e

6a

Socrates: Maybe this, Euthyphro, is why I am being prosecuted for this crime, that whenever someone says such things about the gods, for some reason I find them hard to accept? For this reason, I suppose,

---

1   *the same as itself in every action* That is, there is just one kind of piety—all pious actions have something in common.

2   *Zeus ... his own father ... his own father ...* For the stories of Zeus, Cronos, and Ouranos, see Hesiod, *Theogony*, 154–82 and 453–506.

someone will claim I misbehave. But now if you, with your expertise in such matters, also hold these beliefs, it's surely necessary, I suppose, that we too must accept them—for indeed what *can* we say, we who admit openly that we know nothing about these matters? But before the god of friendship[1] tell me, do you truly believe these things happened like this?

Euthyphro: These and still more amazing things, Socrates, that most people are unaware of.

Socrates: And do you believe there is really a war amongst the gods, with terrible feuds, even, and battles and many other such things, such as are recounted by the poets and the holy artists, and that have been elaborately adorned for us on sacred objects, too, and especially the robe covered with such designs which is brought up to the acropolis at the great Panathenaea?[2] Are we to say that these things are true, Euthyphro?

Euthyphro: Not only these, Socrates, but as I said just now, I could also describe many other things about the gods to you, if you want, which I am sure you will be astounded to hear.

Socrates: I wouldn't be surprised. But you can describe these to me at leisure some other time. For the time being, however, try to state more clearly what I asked you just now, since previously, my friend, you did not teach me well enough when I asked what the pious was but you told me that what you're doing is something pious, prosecuting your father for murder.

Euthyphro: And I spoke the truth, too, Socrates.

Socrates: Perhaps. But in fact, Euthyphro, you say there are many other pious things.

Euthyphro: Indeed there are.

Socrates: So do you remember that I did not request this from you, to teach me one or two of the many pious things, but to teach me the form

---

1   *the god of friendship* Zeus Philios, or Zeus in his aspect of the champion of friendship.
2   *robe ... great Panathenaea?* The Panathenaea was a celebration of Athena's birthday, held annually, with a larger ("great") celebration every four years. A new robe would be presented to the statue of the goddess Athena.

itself by which everything pious is pious? For you said that it's by one form that impious things are somehow impious and pious things pious. Or don't you remember?

e

Euthyphro: I certainly do.

Socrates: So then tell me whatever this form itself is, so that, by looking at it and using it as a paradigm, if you or anyone else do anything of that kind I can say that it is pious, and if it is not of that kind, that it is not.

Euthyphro: Well if that's what you want, Socrates, that's what I'll tell you.

Socrates: That's exactly what I want.

Euthyphro: Well, what is beloved by the gods is pious, and what is not beloved by them is impious.

7a

Socrates: Excellent, Euthyphro! And you have answered in the way I was looking for you to answer. Whether you have done so truly or not, that I don't quite know—but you will obviously spell out how what you say is true.

Euthyphro: Absolutely.

Socrates: Come then, let's look at what we said. An action or a person that is beloved by the gods is pious, while an action or person that is despised by the gods is impious. It is not the same, but the complete opposite, the pious to the impious. Isn't that so?

Euthyphro: Indeed it is.

Socrates: And this seems right?

Euthyphro: I think so, Socrates.

b

Socrates: But wasn't it also said that the gods are at odds with each other and disagree with one another and that there are feuds among them?

Euthyphro: Yes, it was.

Socrates: What is the disagreement about, my good man, that causes hatred and anger? Let's look at it this way. If we disagree, you and I, about quantity, over which of two groups is greater, would our disagreement over this make us enemies and angry with each other, or

c   wouldn't we quickly resolve the issue by resorting to counting?

Euthyphro: Of course.

Socrates: And again, if we disagreed about bigger and smaller, we would quickly put an end to the disagreement by resorting to measurement?

Euthyphro: That's right.

Socrates: And we would weigh with scales, I presume, to reach a decision about heavier and lighter?

Euthyphro: How else?

Socrates: Then what topic, exactly, would divide us and what difference would we be unable to settle such that we would be enemies and angry with one another? Perhaps you don't have an

d   answer at hand, so as I'm talking, see if it's the just and the unjust, the noble and the shameful, and the good and the bad. Isn't it these things that make us enemies of one another, any time that happens, whether to me and you or to any other men, when we quarrel about them and are unable to come to a satisfactory judgment about them?

Euthyphro: It is indeed this disagreement, Socrates, and over these things.

Socrates: And what about the gods, Euthyphro? If they indeed disagree over something, don't they disagree over these very things?

Euthyphro: It's undoubtedly necessary.

e   Socrates: Then some of the gods think different things are just—according to you, worthy Euthyphro—and noble and shameful, and good and bad, since they surely wouldn't be at odds with one another unless they were disagreeing about these things. Right?

Euthyphro: You're right.

Socrates: And so whatever each group thinks is noble and good and just, they also love these things, and they hate the things that are the opposites of these?

Euthyphro: Certainly.

Socrates: Then according to you the things some of them think are just, others think are unjust, and by disagreeing about these things they are at odds and at war with each other. Isn't this so?   8a

Euthyphro: It is.

Socrates: The same things, it seems, are both hated by the gods and loved, and so would be both despised and beloved by them?

Euthyphro: It seems so.

Socrates: And the same things would be both pious and impious, Euthyphro, according to this argument?

Euthyphro: I'm afraid so.

Socrates: So you haven't answered what I was asking, you remarkable man! I didn't ask you for what is both pious and impious at once: what is beloved by the gods is also hated by the gods, as it appears. As a result, Euthyphro, it wouldn't be surprising if in doing what you're   b doing now—punishing your father—you were doing something beloved by Zeus but despised by Cronos and Uranus, and while it is dear to Hephaestus, it is despised by Hera, and if any other god disagrees with another on the subject, your action will also appear to them similarly.

Euthyphro: But I believe, Socrates, that none of the gods will disagree with any other on this matter at least: that any man who has killed another person unjustly need not pay the penalty.

Socrates: What's that? Have you never heard any *man* arguing that someone who killed unjustly or did something else unjustly should not   c pay the penalty?

Euthyphro: There's no end to these arguments, both outside and inside the courts, since people commit so many injustices and do and say anything to escape the punishment.

Socrates: Do they actually agree that they are guilty, Euthyphro, and despite agreeing they nonetheless say that they shouldn't pay the penalty?

Euthyphro: They don't agree on that at all.

d Socrates: So they don't do or say *everything*, since, I think, they don't dare to claim or argue for this: that if they are in fact guilty they should *not* pay the penalty. Rather, I think they claim that they're not guilty. Right?

Euthyphro: That's true.

Socrates: So they don't argue, at least, that the guilty person shouldn't pay the penalty, but perhaps they argue about who the guilty party is and what he did and when.

Euthyphro: That's true.

Socrates: Doesn't the very same thing happen to the gods, too, if indeed, as you said, they are at odds about just and unjust things, some saying that a god commits an injustice against another one, while others deny it? But absolutely no one at all, you remarkable man, either god or human, dares to say that the guilty person need not pay the penalty.

e

Euthyphro: Yes. What you say is true, Socrates, for the most part.

Socrates: But I think that those who quarrel, Euthyphro, both men and gods, if the gods actually quarrel, argue over the particulars of what was done. Differing over a certain action, some say that it was done justly, others that it was done unjustly. Isn't that so?

Euthyphro: Certainly.

9a Socrates: Come now, my dear Euthyphro. So that I can become wiser, teach me too what evidence you have that all gods think the man was killed unjustly—the one who committed murder while he was working for you, and was bound by the master of the man he killed, and died from his bonds before the servant could learn from the interpreters what ought to be done in his case, and is the sort of person on whose behalf it is proper for a son to prosecute his father and make an allegation of murder. Come, try to give me a clear indication of how in this

case all the gods believe beyond doubt that this action is proper. If you b
could show me this satisfactorily I would never stop praising you for
your wisdom.

Euthyphro: But this is probably quite a task, Socrates, though I could
explain it to you very clearly, even so.

Socrates: I understand. It's because you think I'm a slower learner than
the judges, since you could make it clear to *them* in what way these actions are unjust and how the gods all hate such things.

Euthyphro: Very clear indeed, Socrates, if only they would listen to
me when I talk.

Socrates: Of course they'll listen, so long as they think you speak
well. But while you were speaking the following occurred to me: c
I'm thinking to myself, "Even if Euthyphro convincingly shows me
that every god thinks this kind of death is unjust, what more will I
have learned from Euthyphro about what the pious and the impious
are? Because while this particular deed might be despised by the
gods, as is likely, it was already apparent, just a moment ago, that the
pious and impious aren't defined this way, since we saw that what is
despised by the gods is also beloved by them." So I acquit you of
this, Euthyphro. If you want, let us allow that all gods think this is d
unjust and that all of them despise it. But this current correction to
the definition—that what all the gods despise is impious while what
they love is pious, and what some love and some hate is neither or
both—do you want us to now define the pious and the impious in
this way?

Euthyphro: Well, what is stopping us, Socrates?

Socrates: For my part nothing, Euthyphro, but think about whether
adopting this definition will make it easiest for you to teach me what
you promised.

Euthyphro: I do indeed say that the pious is what all the gods love, e
and the opposite, what all gods hate, is impious.

Socrates: Then let's look again, Euthyphro, to see whether it's well
stated. Or will we be content to simply accept our own definition or
someone else's, agreeing that it is right just because somebody says it
is? Or must we examine what the speaker is saying?

Euthyphro: We must examine it. But I'm quite confident that what we have now is well put.

10a   Socrates: We'll soon know better, my good man. Think about this: Is the pious loved by the gods because it's pious, or it is pious because it is loved?

Euthyphro: I don't know what you mean, Socrates.

Socrates: I'll try to express myself more clearly. We speak of something being carried and of carrying, and being led and leading, and being seen and seeing, and so you understand that all of these are different from one another and how they are different?

Euthyphro: I think I understand.

Socrates: So there's a thing loved and different from this there's the thing that loves?

Euthyphro: How could there not be?

b   Socrates: Then tell me whether what is carried is a carried thing because it is carried, or because of something else?

Euthyphro: No, it's because of this.

Socrates: And also what is led because it is led, and what is seen because it is seen?

Euthyphro: Absolutely.

Socrates: So it is not that because it is something seen, it is seen, but the opposite, that because it is seen it is something seen. And it is not because it is something led that it is led, but because it is led it is something led. And it is not because it is something carried that it is carried, but because it is carried, it is something carried. Is it becoming clear
c   what I'm trying to say, Euthyphro? I mean this: that if something becomes or is affected by something, it's not because it is a thing coming to be that it comes to be; but because it comes to be it is a thing coming into being. Nor is it affected by something because it is a thing that is affected; but because it is affected, it is a thing that is being affected. Or don't you agree?

Euthyphro: I do.

Socrates: And is a loved thing either a thing coming to be or a thing affected by something?

Euthyphro: Certainly.

Socrates: And does the same apply to this as to the previous cases: it is not because it is a loved thing that it is loved by those who love it, but it is a loved thing because it is loved?

Euthyphro: Necessarily.

Socrates: So what do we say about the pious, Euthyphro? Precisely   d
that is it loved by all the gods, according to your statement?

Euthyphro: Yes.

Socrates: Is it because of this: that it is pious? Or because of something else?

Euthyphro: No, it's because of that.

Socrates: Because it is pious, then, it is loved, rather than being pious because it is loved?

Euthyphro: It seems so.

Socrates: Then because it loved by the gods it is a loved thing and beloved by the gods?

Euthyphro: How could it not?   e

Socrates: So the beloved is not pious, Euthyphro, nor is the pious beloved by the gods, as you claim, but the one is different from the other.

Euthyphro: How so, Socrates?

Socrates: Because we agree that the pious is loved because of this—that is, because it's pious—and not that it is pious because it is loved. Right?

Euthyphro: Yes.

Socrates: The beloved, on the other hand, because it is loved by gods, is beloved due to this very act of being loved, rather than being loved because it is beloved?

Euthyphro: That's true.

Socrates: But if the beloved and the pious were in fact the same, my
11a dear Euthyphro, then, if the pious were loved because of being the pious, the beloved would be loved because of being the beloved; and again, if the beloved was beloved because of being loved by gods, the pious would also be pious by being loved. But as it is, you see that the two are opposites and are completely different from one another, since the one, because it is loved, is the kind of thing that is loved, while the other is loved because it is the kind of thing that is loved.

So I'm afraid, Euthyphro, that when you were asked what in the world the pious is, you did not want to reveal its nature to me, but wanted to tell me some one of its qualities—that the pious has the qual-
b ity of being loved by all the gods—but as for what it *is*, you did not say at all. So if I am dear to you, don't keep me in the dark but tell me again from the beginning what in the world the pious is. And we won't differ over whether it is loved by the gods or whatever else happens to it, but tell me without delay, what is the pious, and the impious?

Euthyphro: But Socrates, I have no way of telling you what I'm think-ing, because somehow whatever we put forward always wanders off on us and doesn't want to stay where we put it.

Socrates: Your statements, Euthyphro, seem to belong to my ances-
c tor Daedalus.[1] And if I were saying them and putting them forward, perhaps you would be joking about how, on account of my rela-tionship to him, my works made of words run away even on me and don't want to stay wherever a person might put them. But at pres-ent these propositions are yours, and so we have to find some other joke, since they don't want to stay put for you, as even you yourself admit.

---

1   *Daedalus* The statues made by the mythical Daedalus were said to be so lifelike that they appeared to move. Daedalus is most famous for making wings for him-self and his son Icarus to use to escape from Crete.

Euthyphro: It seems to me that pretty much the same joke applies to the statements, Socrates, since I am not the inspiration for their wan-   d
dering off and their refusal to stay in the same place. Rather, it seems to me that you are the Daedalus, since they would stay in place just fine for me, at least.

Socrates: Then I'm afraid, my friend, that I've become more skilled in the craft than the man himself, to the extent that while he could only make his own works move, I can do so to others' works as well as my own. And to my mind this is the most exquisite thing about my skill, that I am unintentionally clever, since I wanted the words to stay put for me and to be fixed motionless more than to have the money of Tan-   e
talos and the skill of Daedalus combined. But enough of this. Since I think you are soft, I myself will help you educate me about the pious. So don't give up the task. See whether you believe that everything pious is necessarily just.

Euthyphro: I do.

Socrates: And is everything just pious? Or is every part of piety just but   12a
the just is not the whole of piety, but some part of it is pious, and some other part is different?

Euthyphro: I can't keep up with what you're saying, Socrates.

Socrates: And yet you are younger than me by at least as much as you are wiser than me! But, as I say, you are spoiled by your abundance of wisdom. Pull yourself together, you blessed man, since what I'm say- ing is not difficult to get your head around. I mean, of course, the op- posite of what the poet meant when he wrote:

> Zeus who created it and who produced all of these

> You do not want to revile; for where there is fear there is also   b
> respect.[1]

I disagree with this statement from the poet. Shall I tell you how?

Euthyphro: Yes indeed.

---

1   *there is also respect* The quotation is from Stanisos' *Cypria*, a collection of tales describing the events prior to the beginning of Homer's *Iliad*.

Socrates: I don't think that "where there is fear there is also respect" since I think many people who fear sickness, poverty and many other things feel fear, but they feel no respect at these things they fear. Don't you think so, too?

Euthyphro: Certainly.

Socrates: Where there is respect, though, there is also fear, for is there anyone who feels respect and is ashamed at some act who doesn't also
c   feel fear and dread a reputation for cowardice?

Euthyphro: He does indeed dread it.

Socrates: So it's not right to claim that "where there is fear there is also respect," for respect is not in fact everywhere fear is, but instead where there is respect there is also fear. Because I think fear covers more than respect since respect is a part of fear, just as oddness is a part of number, so that it's not the case that where there is number there is also oddness, but where there is oddness, there is also number. Do you follow now, at least?

Euthyphro: I certainly do.

Socrates: This is the kind of thing I was talking about earlier when I was questioning you: where there is justice, is there also piety? Or is
d   it that where there is piety, there is also justice, but piety is not every-where justice is, since piety is a part of justice? Do you think we should speak in this way or in some other?

Euthyphro: No, in this way. I think you're speaking properly.

Socrates: Then see what follows this: if the pious is a part of the just, we must, it seems, discover what part of the just the pious might be. If, to go back to what we were just discussing, you now asked me something such as what part of number the even is, and what kind of number it happens to be, I would say that it would be the number that can be divided into two equal and not unequal parts.[1] Doesn't it seem so to you?

Euthyphro: It does.

---

1   *divided into two equal and not unequal parts* Literally "isosceles and not scalene," presumably because isosceles triangles have two equal legs.

Socrates: So try to teach me in this way, Euthyphro, what sort of part e
of the just piety is, so that we can also tell Meletus not to do us wrong
and charge me with impiety, since I have already learned enough from
you about what is holy and what is pious and what is not.

Euthyphro: It seems to me now, Socrates, that holiness and piety is
the part of justice concerned with attending to the gods, while the re-
maining part of justice is concerned with attending to human beings.

Socrates: I think you put that well, Euthyphro. But I still need just one 13a
small thing: I don't know quite what you mean by "attending." Surely
you don't mean that attending to the gods is like the other kinds of attending, even though we do say so. We say, for example, that not
everybody knows how to attend to a horse, just the horse-trainer.
Right?

Euthyphro: Certainly.

Socrates: Since horse-training is attending to horses?

Euthyphro: Yes.

Socrates: And no one but the dog-trainer knows how to attend to
dogs?

Euthyphro: Right.

Socrates: And dog-training is attending to dogs?

Euthyphro: Yes. b

Socrates: And cattle-herding is to cattle?

Euthyphro: Absolutely.

Socrates: Naturally, then, piety and holiness are to the gods, Euthyphro? That's what you say?

Euthyphro: I do.

Socrates: Then does all attending bring about the same effect? Something of the following sort: the good and benefit of what is

attended to, in just the way you see that horses, when attended to by horse-trainers, are benefited and become better? Or don't you think they are?

Euthyphro: They are.

c   Socrates: And dogs by the dog-trainer somehow, and cattle by the cattle-herder, and all the others similarly? Or do you think the attending is aimed at harming what is attended to?

Euthyphro: By Zeus, I do not.

Socrates: But at benefiting them?

Euthyphro: How could it not be?

Socrates: And since piousness is attending to the gods, does it benefit the gods and make the gods better? Do you agree to this, that whenever one does something pious it results in some improvement of the gods?

Euthyphro: By Zeus, no, I don't.

Socrates: Nor did I think that that's what you meant, Euthyphro—far from it, in fact—and that's why I was asking what you really meant by
d   "attending to the gods," because I didn't think you mean this kind of thing.

Euthyphro: And you're right, Socrates. Because I mean no such thing.

Socrates: Alright then. But what kind of attending to the gods would piousness be, then?

Euthyphro: The kind, Socrates, when slaves attend to their masters.

Socrates: I understand. It would be a kind of service to gods, it seems.

Euthyphro: Certainly.

Socrates: Can you tell me about service to doctors, what end result is such service aimed at? Don't you think it's at health?

Euthyphro: I do.

Socrates: And what about service to shipbuilders? What end result is   e
that service aimed at?

Euthyphro: Clearly it's aimed at a ship, Socrates.

Socrates: And service to house-builders, I suppose, is aimed at houses?

Euthyphro: Yes.

Socrates: Tell me then, best of men, what end result is service to the
gods aimed at? It's obvious that you know, since you claim to have
the finest religious knowledge—of any human, at least.

Euthyphro: And as a matter of fact, Socrates, I speak the truth.

Socrates: So tell me, by Zeus, what in the world is that magnificent
task which the gods accomplish by using us as servants?

Euthyphro: Many fine tasks, Socrates.

Socrates: Well, and so do the generals, my friend. But nevertheless   14a
one could easily say what their key purpose is: that they achieve vic-
tory in war. Is that not so?

Euthyphro: How else could it be?

Socrates: And I think the farmers accomplish many fine tasks. And yet
their key purpose is nourishment from the soil.

Euthyphro: Very much so.

Socrates: So what, then, about the many fine things that the gods accomplish? What is the key purpose of their labor?

Euthyphro: As I said a little earlier, Socrates, it is a great task to learn   b
exactly how all these things are. But I will put it for you generally: if
a man knows how to speak and act pleasingly to the gods in his prayers
and sacrifices, those are pious, and such things preserve both his own
home and the common good of the city. But the opposites of these
pleasing things are unholy, and they obviously overturn and destroy
everything.

Socrates: If you were willing, Euthyphro, you could have told me the heart of what I was asking much more briefly. But in fact you are not eager to teach me, that much is clear—since now when you were just about to do so, you turned away. If you had given your answer, I would already have a satisfactory understanding of piousness from you. But for the present, the lover must follow his beloved wherever he might lead. So what do you say the pious and piousness are, again? Aren't you saying it's a certain kind of knowledge, of how to sacrifice and pray?

Euthyphro: I am.

Socrates: And sacrificing is giving to the gods, while praying is making a request of the gods?

Euthyphro: Very much so, Socrates.

Socrates: Based on this, piousness would be knowledge of making requests and giving things to the gods?

Euthyphro: You have understood my meaning very well, Socrates.

Socrates: It's because I am eager for your wisdom, my friend, and pay close attention to it, so that nothing you might say falls to the ground. But tell me, what is this service to the gods? You say it is making requests of them and giving to them?

Euthyphro: I do.

Socrates: And proper requests would be requests for what we need from them, asking them for these things?

Euthyphro: What else?

Socrates: And again, giving properly would be giving what they happen to want from us, to give these things to them in return? Since to give a gift by giving someone what he has no need of would not be too skillful, I suppose.

Euthyphro: That's true, Socrates.

Socrates: So piousness for gods and humans, Euthyphro, would be some skill of trading with one another?

Euthyphro: If naming it that way is sweeter for you, call it "trading."

Socrates: As far as I'm concerned, nothing is sweeter unless it is true. Tell me, how do the gods benefit from the gifts they receive from us? What they give us is clear to everyone, since every good we have was given by them. But what they receive from us, what good is it? Or do we fare so much better than them in the trade that we get everything that's good from them, while they get nothing from us?   15a

Euthyphro: But do you think, Socrates, that the gods are benefited by what they receive from us?

Socrates: Well then what in the world would they be, Euthyphro, these gifts from us to the gods?

Euthyphro: What else, do you think, but honor and admiration and, as I said just now, gratitude?

Socrates: So being shown gratitude is what's pious, Euthyphro, but it   b is neither beneficial to the gods nor dear to them?

Euthyphro: I think it is dear to them above everything else.

Socrates: So the pious is once again, it seems, what is dear to gods.

Euthyphro: Very much so.

Socrates: Are you at all surprised, when you say such things, that your words seem not to stand still but to move around? And you accuse me of making them move around like a Daedalus when you yourself are much more skilled than Daedalus, even making things go around in circles? Or don't you see that our discussion has gone around and arrived back at the same place? You remember, no doubt, that   c previously the pious and the beloved by the gods seemed to us not to be the same but different from one another. Or don't you remember?

Euthyphro: I certainly do.

Socrates: Well, don't you realize now that you're saying that what is dear to the gods is pious? But this is nothing other than what is beloved by the gods, isn't it?

Euthyphro: It certainly is.

Socrates: So either what we decided then was wrong, or, if we were right then, we are wrong now.

Euthyphro: So it seems.

Socrates: Then we must examine again from the beginning what the pious is, as I am determined not to give up until I understand it. Do not
d   scorn me, but by applying your mind in every way, tell me the truth now more than ever. Because you know it if anybody does and, like Proteus,[1] you cannot be released until you tell me. Because unless you knew clearly about the pious and impious there is no way you would ever have, on behalf of a hired laborer, tried to pursue your aging father for murder. Instead you would have been afraid before the gods, and ashamed before men, to run the risk of conducting this matter im-
e   properly. But as it is, I am sure that you think you have clear knowledge of the pious and the impious. So tell me, great Euthyphro, and do not conceal what you think it is.

Euthyphro: Well, some other time, Socrates, because I'm in a hurry to get somewhere and it's time for me to go.

Socrates: What a thing to do, my friend! By leaving, you have cast me down from a great hope I had: that I would learn from you what is pious and what is not, and moreover would free myself from Mele-
16a tus's charge by showing him that, thanks to Euthyphro, I had already become wise in religious matters and that I would no longer speak carelessly and innovate about these things due to ignorance, and most of all that I would live better for the rest of my life.

---

1   *Proteus* A mythical sea god who could change shape. Menelaus had to hold on to Proteus as he changed shape in order to get him to prophesy. (See Homer, *Odyssey* 4.398–463.)

Apology

Introduction

The *Apology* is so called, not because Socrates is the least bit apologetic (in the modern sense), but as a transliteration of the Greek word *apologia*, which means a speech in defense of one's beliefs or behavior. It is Plato's depiction of the speech that Socrates made at his trial, in response to accusations of impiety and the corruption of the youth of Athens.

It has three parts. The first is Socrates' speech in his own defense. Socrates was unsuccessful, and the jury voted to convict him. The second speech is Socrates' proposal for what his punishment should be (see the general introduction for more information on Athenian trial procedures). In this he also fails to persuade the jury, and he is sentenced to death. The final speech—which would not have been part of the court procedure—comprises his reflections to his friends before he is led off to await his execution.

Apology

How you were affected, men of Athens,[1] by my accusers, I do not   17a
know. But I, even I myself almost forgot who I was because of them,
so persuasively did they speak. And yet they have said practically nothing true. I was especially amazed by one of the many lies they told, the one in which they said that you should take care not to be deceived by me because I am a skilled speaker. Their lack of shame—since they   b
will be exposed immediately by what I do, when I show myself not to be a clever speaker at all—this seems to me to be most disgraceful of them. Unless of course they mean to call "clever" someone who speaks the truth. Because if they mean this, then I would indeed admit—not in the way they do—that I am an orator.

---

1   *men of Athens* The proper form of address is "judges" or "gentlemen of the
     jury," which Socrates uses later. (See 40a.)

So, as I say, these men have said little or nothing that is true, whereas from me you will hear the whole truth. Not, by Zeus, beautified speeches like theirs, men of Athens, and not ornamented with fine phrases and words, but you will hear me say the words that come to me spoken at random—for I believe what I say is just—and let none of you expect otherwise. After all, it would surely not be fitting, gentlemen, for someone of my age to come before you composing speeches, as it might be for a young man. And this most of all, men of Athens, I beg and request of you: if in these speeches you hear me defending myself in the language I also typically use in the marketplace by the tables, where many of you have heard me, as well as elsewhere, don't be surprised and don't make a disturbance because of it. Because this is exactly how it is: I have now come before the court for the first time, at seventy years of age.[1] So I am simply a stranger to the manner of speech here. And so, just as you would certainly have sympathy for me if I actually happened to be a stranger and spoke in the accent and manner in which I had been raised, I now particularly ask you for this just request, at least as it seems to me, to disregard my manner of speech—maybe it's better, maybe it's worse—and to consider only the following and pay attention to it: whether I say just things or not. For this is the virtue of a judge, while of an orator it is to speak the truth.

It is right for me to defend myself, men of Athens, first against the earliest untrue accusations made against me and the earliest accusers, and then against the later accusations and the later accusers. For many of my accusers came to you many years ago now, saying nothing true, and I fear these more than Anytus and his friends,[2] though indeed they are dangerous too. But these men are more dangerous, gentlemen, the ones who, taking most of you aside from childhood, influenced you and made accusations against me that are not in fact true: that there is a certain Socrates, a clever man, a student of things in the sky who has investigated everything under the earth, and who makes the weaker speech the stronger. These people, men of Athens, having spread this allegation, are my fearsome accusers, for those who have heard them think that the people who study these things do not acknowledge the

c

d

18a

b

c

---

1   *seventy* The year is 399 BCE, which puts Socrates' birth at 469 BCE. Other references to Socrates' age are made by him at 17c, 25d, 34e, 37d, *Crito* 43b, 49a, 52e.

2   *Anytus and his friends* His friends were Meletus and Lycon; the three of them were prosecuting. The leader of the prosecution was Meletus, a young man who probably held a grudge against Socrates; Anytus hated the Sophists and probably regarded Socrates as one of them; Lycon was a rhetorician. Anytus is mentioned in particular because he was the most politically influential of these, having played an important part in the restoration of Athenian democracy.

gods either. Moreover, these accusers are numerous and have been making accusations for a long time now. And what's more, they spoke to you at an age when you would be liable to believe them—some of you being children and youths—crudely making accusations against an absent person with no one else to make a rebuttal.

What is most unreasonable is that one can't know and name the names of these people, except if one happens to be a comic playwright.[1] These people who misled you with envy and slander—and others who, having themselves been persuaded, then persuade others—all of these are hardest to deal with. For it is not possible to summon them here to court or to cross-examine any of them, but it is necessary to defend myself just as if shadow-boxing, and conduct a cross-examination without anyone responding. So you too must accept that my accusers are twofold, as I said, those who accused me recently and those whom I mentioned from long ago, and believe that I must first defend myself against the latter. For you heard their accusations against me earlier and much more often than those of the later people.

Well then. I must make a defense, men of Athens, and in such a short time must try to banish this prejudice from you that you have held for a long time. I would like it to turn out this way—that I will succeed in defending myself—if that would be better for both you and me. But I think this is difficult, and just what it is I'm attempting doesn't escape me at all. Nevertheless, let the case proceed in whatever way the god favors; I must obey the law and make my defense.

Let us consider, then, from the beginning, what the accusation is, from which the prejudice against me arose that Meletus believed when he brought this charge against me. Well then. What precisely did the accusers say when they accused me? Just as if they were charging me, it is necessary to read out their indictment: "Socrates is guilty of meddling, of inquiring into things under the earth and in the heavens, of making the weaker speech the stronger, and of teaching these very things"—something like this. For even you yourselves have seen these things in the comedy of Aristophanes, a certain Socrates being carried around up there,[2] insisting that he walks on air and spouting

---

1   *a comic playwright* In his play *Clouds* of 423, Aristophanes had portrayed a Socrates who was head of a "Thinkery" of students engaged in natural science and cosmological speculation, as well as in argumentation. Aristophanes is named in 19c. His caricature of Socrates seems to combine two types: the natural scientist and the sophist.

2   *Socrates being carried around up there* In the play, the satire of Socrates' desire to inquire into higher things is given physical form through the depiction of Socrates in a hanging basket.

off a lot of other nonsense that I do not claim to know anything about, either great or small. I don't speak in order to dishonor such knowledge, if someone is wise about such things—I hope I am not somehow prosecuted by Meletus on such great charges—but in fact I have

d   nothing to do with them, men of Athens, and I call on the majority of you as witnesses, and I expect you to teach and inform one another, those of you who have ever heard me in conversation—and this includes many of you. Tell one another if any of you heard me ever discussing such things, either a lot or a little. And from this you will realize that the same is true of the other things that the many say about me.

But in fact none of them is the case. And indeed, if you have heard

e   from anyone that I endeavor to teach people and make money, this is not true. Though again, I think that it is a fine thing if an individual is able to teach people,[1] such as Gorgias of Leontini and Prodicus of Chios and Hippias of Elis. For each of these people, gentlemen, going into each of the cities, to the young—who could associate with whomever they want from their own citizens for free—they convince

20a   them to leave their company and join them, paying them money, and to feel grateful besides!

For that matter, there is currently another wise man, from Paros, whom I have discovered is in town because I happened to meet a man who has paid more money to sophists than all the others combined, Callias, son of Hipponicus. So I asked him—because he has two sons—"Callias," I said, "If colts or calves had been born to you as

b   sons, we could find and hire a trainer who would make them well-bred with respect to the appropriate virtue; he would be some horse-trainer or farmer. But as it is, since they are humans, whom do have in mind to hire as a trainer for them? Who is knowledgeable about such virtue, of the human being and of the citizen? Because I assume you have looked into it, since you have sons. Is there someone," I said, "or not?" "Certainly," said he. "Who?" I said, "And where from? And for how much does he teach?" "Evenus, Socrates," he said, "from Paros, for

c   five mina."[2] And I considered Evenus blessed, if he really has this skill and teaches for such a sweet-sounding price. I at any rate would be proud of myself and be boastful, if I knew these things. But in fact I don't know them, men of Athens.

---

1   *able to teach people*   The names given are all names of sophists (20a).

2   *five mina*   (See also 38b for "a mina of silver".) A mina was 100 silver drachmas (see 26e, 36b), and a drachma was equivalent to 6 obols. Daily earnings ranged from 2–6 obols. Admission to the theater was 2 obols. Pay for being a judge (jury duty) was 2 obols.

Perhaps some one of you might respond, "But Socrates, what is *your* profession? Where have these slanders against you come from? For surely it's not by busying yourself with the usual things that so much hearsay and talk has arisen, but by doing something different from most people. Then tell us what it is, so that we don't judge your case rashly." The person who says this seems to me to speak justly, and I will try to show you what it is, precisely, that won me this reputation and notoriety.   d

Listen, then. And while I will perhaps appear to some of you to be joking, rest assured that I will tell you the whole truth. For I, men of Athens, have acquired this reputation due to nothing other than a certain wisdom. What sort of wisdom is this? Quite likely it is human wisdom. There's a good chance that I actually have this kind of wisdom, while those men I was speaking of just now might perhaps be wise with a wisdom more than human—or I don't know how I should put it, for I certainly don't have it, and whoever says so is lying and is saying it to slander me. But don't interrupt me, men of Athens, not even if I strike you as talking big. The story I will tell you is not my own, but I will refer you to a trustworthy source for what I say, because regarding whether it is wisdom of a sort and of what sort it is I will present to you as my witness the god in Delphi.[1]   e

You know Chaerephon, I presume. He was a companion of mine   21a
from youth and a comrade of yours in the democracy and joined you in the recent exile[2] and returned with you. And you know how Chaerephon was, how zealous he was about whatever he pursued, and so for example when he went to Delphi he was so bold as to ask this— and, as I say, don't interrupt, gentlemen—he asked if there was any- one wiser than me. The Pythia then replied that no one was wiser. And his brother here will bear witness to you about these things, since he himself has died.

Think about why I am bringing this up: it's because I'm going to   b
teach you where the prejudice against me came from. Because when I heard this I pondered in the following way: "Whatever does the god mean? And what riddle is he posing? For I am not aware of being wise in anything great or small. What in the world does he mean, then, when

---

1   *the god in Delphi* At Delphi one could ask questions of the god Apollo via his
      oracle, a priestess known as the Pythia.

2   *in the democracy ... the recent exile* Athens was subject to violent political tur-
      moil between rival factions who wanted to restrict the ruling positions to a small
      number (oligarchs) or broaden it to more (democrats). See also 32c. For details
      of the exile and return, see the Introduction, pp. 15–16.

he says that I am wisest? For certainly he does not lie; he is not permitted to." And for a long time I puzzled over his meaning.

Then, very reluctantly, I embarked on a sort of trial of him. I went to one of the people who are thought to be wise, hoping to refute the oracle there if anywhere, and reply to its pronouncement: "This man here is wiser than me, though you said I was." So, scrutinizing this fellow—there's no need to refer to him by name; he was one of the politicians I had this sort of experience with when I examined him, men of Athens—in talking with him it seemed to me that while this man was considered to be wise both by many other people and especially by himself, he was not. And so I tried to show him that he took himself to be wise, but was not. As a result I became hated by this man and by many of those present.

And so, as I was going away, I was thinking to myself, "I am at least wiser than this man. It's likely that neither of us knows anything worthwhile, but whereas he thinks he knows something when he doesn't know it, I, when I don't know something, don't think I know it either. It's likely, then, that by this I am indeed wiser than him in some small way, that I don't think myself to know what I don't know." Next, I went to another one of the people thought to be wiser than him and things seemed the same to me, and so I made an enemy of that man as well as of many others.

So, after this, I now went to one after another, realizing with pain and fear that I was becoming hated. But nevertheless I thought it necessary to consider the god's oracle to be of the utmost importance, so I had to continue going to all of the people thought to know something, investigating the meaning of the oracle. And by the dog, men of Athens, because I must tell you the truth, my experience was really something like the following: in my divine search those held in highest esteem seemed to me to be lacking just about the most, while others thought to be poorer were better men as far as wisdom is concerned.

I have to represent my wanderings to you as though I were undertaking various labors[1] only to find that the oracle was quite irrefutable. After the politicians I went to the poets, including those of tragedies and those of dithyrambs[2] and others, so that there I would catch myself being more ignorant than them. Reading the works which I thought they had really labored over, I would ask them what they meant, so

---

1   *labors* Alluding to the labors of Heracles, a series of difficult tasks the mythological hero performed as penance.
2   *dithyrambs* Hymns to the god Dionysus, sung by a chorus.

that at the same time I might also learn something from them. I am ashamed to tell you the truth, gentlemen, but nevertheless it must be told. Practically anybody present, so to speak, could have better explained what they had written. And so, as before, I quickly realized the following about the poets: that they do not write what they write because of their wisdom but because they have a certain nature and are possessed, like the seers and fortune-tellers, who also say many fine things but know nothing about what they're saying. It seemed clear to me that the poets had had a similar experience. And at once I understood that, because of their writing, they thought themselves to be the wisest of all men even about other things, but they weren't. And so I departed from them thinking that I was superior to them in the same way as I was to the politicians.

c

So finally I went to the crafters, because I was aware that while I knew practically nothing, I knew that I would find that they knew many fine things. And in this I was not mistaken—they knew things I didn't and in this they were wiser than me. But, men of Athens, the noble crafters seemed to me to have the same flaw that the poets also had. Because each of them performed his craft well, he considered himself to be most wise about the greatest things—and this sour note of theirs overshadowed their wisdom. And so I asked myself on behalf of the oracle whether I would prefer to be just as I am—neither being at all wise in the ways that they are wise nor ignorant in the ways they are ignorant—or to be both, as they are. And I answered myself and the oracle that it would be best for me to be as I am.

d

e

As a result of this quest, men of Athens, a lot of hatred developed against me, and of the most difficult and oppressive kind, such that from it many slanders arose, and I gained this reputation for being wise. For on each occasion the bystanders thought that I myself was wise about the subject on which I was examining the other person. But in fact it's likely, gentlemen, that in truth the god is wise, and by this pronouncement he means the following: that human wisdom is worth little or nothing. And he appears to be using me as an example, speaking of this man Socrates and even using my name, just as if he said, "Human beings, he among you is wisest who knows like Socrates that he is actually worthless with respect to wisdom." That's why, both then and now, I go around in accordance with the god, searching and making inquiries of anyone, citizen or stranger, whom I think to be wise. And if I then learn that he isn't, I assist the god and show him that he is not wise. And because of this busyness I lack the time to participate in any public affairs worth mentioning or any private business, but I am in great poverty because of my service to the god.

23a

b

c

Furthermore, the young people follow me around of their own accord, those with the most leisure, the sons of the very wealthy. They
delight in hearing me examine people and they often imitate me, having a go at examining others afterwards. And, I think, they discover a
great number of people who think they know something but know little or nothing. As a result, the people who are examined by them then
d   grow angry with me, but not themselves, and they say that Socrates is
a most vile person and corrupts the young. And whenever anyone asks
them, "By doing what and by teaching what?", they have nothing to
say and do not know, but, so as to not appear at a loss, they say these
things that are handy against all philosophers, about "the heavenly
things and the things under the earth" and "not acknowledging the
gods" and "making the weaker speech the stronger." I believe it's because they don't want to tell the truth, that they are obviously pre-
e   tending to know something even though they know nothing. Since
they are ambitious and impetuous, I think, and there are many of them
and they speak about me ruthlessly and persuasively, they have filled
up your ears, badmouthing me violently for a long time. On the
strength of this, Meletus attacked me along with Anytus and Lycon,
Meletus complaining on behalf of the writers, Anytus on behalf of the
24a   crafters and the politicians, and Lycon on behalf of the orators.

And so, as I said in the beginning, I would be amazed if I could rid
you of this slander in such a short time, since it has become so powerful. This, I assure you, men of Athens, is the truth, and in speaking
I conceal nothing, either big or small, nor hold anything back. Indeed
I am quite aware that I am hated on account of these very things, which
is an indication that I tell the truth, and that this is the slander against
me and that these are the causes. And if you inquire into these things,
b   either now or later, this is what you'll find.

Concerning the charges of my initial accusers, let this defense before you be enough. Next I will try to defend myself against Meletus,
the good and patriotic man, as he says, and the later accusers. And
once more, as though they are different accusers, let's take up their indictment in turn. It goes something like this: he says Socrates is guilty
of corrupting the young and not acknowledging the gods that the city
c   does, but other strange spiritual things. The complaint is something
along these lines. Let's examine this complaint point by point.

He says that I am guilty of corrupting the young. But I say, men of
Athens, that Meletus is guilty, that he jokes in earnest, carelessly bringing a person to trial, pretending to be serious about and to trouble himself over various matters, none of which was ever an interest of his.
This is how it is, as I will try to demonstrate.

Socrates: Here, Meletus, do tell me: don't you take making the   d
young as good as possible to be your highest priority?

Meletus: I certainly do.

Socrates: Come now, tell these men, who makes them better? It's
clear that you know. It's certainly a concern of yours, since upon dis-
covering the one who corrupts them—me, as you claim—you bring
me in front of these people here and accuse me. Come, state who is the
one who makes them better and reveal to them who it is.... You see,
Meletus, that you are silent and unable to speak? Doesn't it seem
shameful to you, and sufficient proof of exactly what I'm claiming,
that it meant nothing to you? So tell us, my good man, who makes
them better?

Meletus: The laws.

Socrates: But that's not what I'm asking, best of men, but what   e
man, whoever knows this very thing—the laws—in the first place?

Meletus: These men, Socrates, the judges.

Socrates: What do you mean, Meletus? These men can educate the
young and make them better?

Meletus: Definitely.

Socrates: All of them, or some can and others can't?

Meletus: All of them.

Socrates: Well done, by Hera! And what a great number of bene-
factors you speak of. What next? Do these listeners[1] make them bet-   25a
ter or not?

Meletus: These too.

Socrates: Who else? The councilors?

Meletus: The councilors too.

Socrates: Well then, Meletus, surely those in the assembly, the as-
semblymen, they don't corrupt the young people? So do they all make
them better, too?

Meletus: These too.

Socrates: Every Athenian, it seems, makes them fine and good except for me, and I alone corrupt them. Is this what you mean?

Meletus: That's exactly what I mean.

Socrates: You charge me with a great misfortune. But answer me:
do you think it's like this with horses? That everyone makes them   b
better, while one person is their corrupter? Or isn't it the complete
opposite of this: one individual can make them better—or very few,
the horse-trainers—while the many corrupt the horses if they deal

---

1   *these listeners* Those attending Socrates' trial; ordinary Athenian citizens.

with them and use them? Isn't this how it is, Meletus, concerning both horses and every other animal? ... It certainly is, whether you and Anytus agree or disagree. It would be a great blessing for the young if only a single person corrupted them, and all the others benefited them. But, Meletus, you have sufficiently demonstrated that you never before cared about the young, and you clearly reveal your indifference in that you have given no thought at all to the matters you indict me on.

c

Still, before Zeus, Meletus, tell us whether it is better to live among good citizens or wicked ones? ... Answer, my good man—I'm not asking anything difficult, you know. Don't the wicked always do something bad to those who are constantly closest to them, while the good do something good?

Meletus: Certainly.

d

Socrates: But is there anyone who wishes to be harmed by those he associates with rather than to be helped? ... Keep answering, my good man, for the law also requires you to answer. Is there anyone who wants to be harmed?

Meletus: Of course not.

Socrates: Come then, do you bring me here on charges of intentionally or unintentionally corrupting the young and making them worse?

Meletus: Intentionally, I say.

Socrates: What then, Meletus? Are you so much wiser at your age than I am at mine that you know that the wicked always do something bad to those who are very close to them, and the good do good, while I, on the other hand, have fallen into such great ignorance that I don't also know this—that if I make one of my associates bad, I risk being harmed by him? And so I would do this great evil intentionally, as you claim?

e

26a

I don't believe you, Meletus, and I think that no one else does. And either I do not corrupt, or if I do corrupt, I do so unintentionally, and so you are lying either way. If I corrupt unintentionally, the procedure is not to prosecute me here for such offenses, but to take me aside privately and teach and admonish me, since it is clear that if I learn, I will cease doing what I do unintentionally. You, however, fled from me and were unwilling to associate with me and teach me, but prosecuted me here, where the procedure is to prosecute those who need punishment rather than instruction.

And so, men of Athens, what I was saying is now clear, that Meletus never troubled himself about these matters in the slightest.

b

Nevertheless, tell us, Meletus, how do I corrupt the young, according to you? Or rather, isn't it clear from the indictment you wrote that

I corrupt them by teaching them not to acknowledge the gods that the city recognizes, but other strange spiritual things? Don't you say that I corrupt them by teaching these things?

Meletus: That's absolutely what I'm saying.

Socrates: But by the gods, Meletus, the very gods that the discussion is currently about, speak even more clearly to me and these people here, because I can't tell whether you mean that I teach the young   c
to believe that there are some gods—and so I believe there are gods and am not entirely godless nor guilty of this—not, however, the gods that the city believes in but others, and this is what you prosecute me for, that they are different, or, whether you mean that I do not acknowledge gods at all, and teach this to others?

Meletus: That's what I mean, that you don't acknowledge the gods at all.

Socrates: Incredible Meletus, why do you say that? I don't believe   d
the sun, or even the moon, to be gods,[1] like other men do?

Meletus: No, by Zeus, judges, since he says that the sun is a stone and the moon is earth.

Socrates: Do you think you are prosecuting Anaxagoras, my dear Meletus? Do you have so much contempt for these men, and think them to be so unfamiliar with literature that they do not know that the books of Anaxagoras of Clazomenae are full of such claims? And what's more, do you think that the young learn these things from me, which they can buy sometimes for a drachma, at most, on the floor of   e
the agora and can mock Socrates for, if he pretends they are his, especially when they are so distinctive? By Zeus, is this how I appear to you? Believing that there are no gods?

Meletus: You certainly don't, by Zeus; none whatsoever.

Socrates: You are unbelievable, Meletus, and are so even to yourself, I think. For the man seems to me, men of Athens, to be exceedingly arrogant and uncontrolled, and clumsily lodged this indictment out of hubris and lack of discipline and youthful zeal. He appears to be testing me, as though setting a riddle: "Will the wise Socrates realize   27a
that I am being facetious and contradicting myself, or will I deceive him and the other listeners?" For it looks to me as though he is saying contradictory things in his indictment, just as if he said "Socrates is guilty of not acknowledging the gods, and of acknowledging the gods." This is just like a riddler.

Now join me in examining, gentlemen, in what way he seems to be saying these things. And you, Meletus, answer us. And as I begged   b

---

1   *I don't believe ... to be gods* Sun and moon worship were common in Greece.

of you all at the beginning, remember not to interrupt if I speak in my customary way.

Is there anyone, Meletus, who believes there are human matters, but does not believe in humans? ... Gentlemen, make him answer and not digress about other things. Is there anyone who does not believe there are horses, but believes there are equestrian matters? Or that there are not flute-players but there are flute-playing matters? ... There is not, best of men—since you are unwilling to answer I will answer on behalf of you and these others. But at least answer the next question:

c   Is there anyone who believes there are spiritual matters but does not believe there are spirits?

Meletus: There is not.

Socrates: How delightful, that you answered reluctantly when compelled by these men. And so you say that I acknowledge and teach about spirits, and whether they be novel or old I at any rate believe in spiritual matters, according to your accusation, and you even swear this in the indictment. But if I believe in spiritual matters, surely it is unavoidably necessary that I believe in spirits too. Isn't that so? ... Of course it is. I take it that you agree, since you're not answering. Now,

d   don't we think the spirits are either gods or the children of gods? Do you agree or not?

Meletus: Yes indeed.

Socrates: Well then, since I believe in spirits, as you say, then if, on the one hand, the spirits are gods of some sort, this would be what I am claiming you are riddling and being facetious about, saying that while I don't believe in gods, at the same time again I do believe in gods, since I indeed believe in spirits.

If, on the other hand, the spirits are certain illegitimate children of gods—either by nymphs or by some others that they're said to come from—who among men would think the children of gods exist, but

e   not gods? Similarly, it would be strange if someone believed in the children of horses, or of asses too, namely mules, but did not believe in horses and asses.

And so, Meletus, it must be that you brought this indictment in order to test us about these things, or were at a loss as to what true crime you might charge me with. How you could persuade anyone with even a little intelligence that the same man does not believe in

28a   both spiritual and divine matters, or again, that this same man believes in neither spirits nor gods nor heroes—it's not possible!

And so, men of Athens, it seems to me that it doesn't take much of a defense to show I am not guilty of what Meletus charges me with, and even this is enough. What I said earlier, on the other hand—that I incurred a great hatred and from many people—you know well to be

true. This is what convicts me, if indeed it convicts me, and not Meletus or Anytus, but the slander and malice of many people. And I know
that these people have convicted, and will convict, many other good
men; there is no fear that they will stop with me.　　　　　　　　　b

Perhaps then someone might say, "Aren't you ashamed, Socrates,
that you engaged in the kind of practice that now places you at risk of
dying?" In reply to this I would justly say, "You do not speak well,
Sir, if you think a man who is worth anything should take the risk of
living or dying into account, rather than looking only to this: whether
when he acts he acts justly or unjustly, and does the deeds of a good
man or a bad one." For those demigods who met their ends in Troy　c
would be fools according to you, especially the son of Thetis,[1] who
thought so little of the risk in comparison with enduring some disgrace
that, when his mother, a god, told him, when he was eager to kill Hector, something like this, as I recall: "Son, if you avenge the slaying of
your comrade Patroclus[2] and kill Hector, you will be killed—because
immediately after Hector," she said, "your fate is at hand," he, hearing this, belittled death and the danger and feared much more living as　d
a coward and not avenging his friends. He said, "May I die at once,
having served justice to the unjust, and not remain here, a laughing
stock by the curved ships, a burden upon the earth." Do you think he
cared about death or danger?

This is how it is, men of Athens, in reality. Wherever someone positions himself, thinking it to be for the best, or is positioned by his
commander, he must, it seems to me, remain there and face the danger, and not put death or anything else ahead of disgrace. I would have
done a terrible thing, men of Athens, if, when positioned by the offi-　e
cers, those whom you elected to command me at Potideia and Amphipolis and Delium,[3] I remained where these men stationed me and
risked dying, just like anyone else, but when stationed by the god, as
I believed and accepted—required to live my life seeking wisdom and
examining both myself and others—I had abandoned my station for　29a
fear of death or anything else. That would be terrible, and truly under
such circumstances someone could justly bring me to court for not believing that there are gods, defying the oracle and fearing death and
thinking myself to be wise when I am not.

1　*son of Thetis*　The son of Thetis is Achilles. His reply to his mother's prophecy is
　　from *Iliad* 18.98.
2　*Hector ... Patroclus*　In the *Iliad*, Hector is a prince of Troy who kills Achilles'
　　comrade, Patroclus, in battle.
3　*Potideia and Amphipolis and Delium*　Part of the Peloponnesian War (431–404
　　BCE) between the Athenian empire and a league led by Sparta, these were battles
　　in which Socrates fought as a citizen-soldier.

Indeed, to fear death, gentlemen, is nothing other than to regard oneself as wise when one is not; for it is to regard oneself as knowing what one does not know. No one knows whether death is not the greatest of all the goods for man, but they fear it as if they knew it to be the greatest of evils. And indeed, how could this ignorance not be reproachable, the ignorance of believing one knows what one does not know? But I, gentlemen, am perhaps superior to the majority of men to this extent and in this regard, and if indeed I seem to be wiser in any way than anyone, it would be in this, that I am not so certain about how things are in Hades and I do not think that I know.

b

But wrongdoing and defiance of one's superiors, whether god or man, *that* I know to be evil and shameful. So I will never fear nor flee things that for all I know could turn out to be good, rather than the evils that I know to be evil. So if you now acquitted me—rejecting Anytus, who said that either I should not have been brought here to trial in the first place, or, now that I have, executing me is unavoidable, and who tells you that if I were acquitted, your sons, practicing what Socrates teaches, will at once be thoroughly corrupted—if, referring to this, you said to me, "Socrates, we are not at present persuaded by Anytus and we acquit you but on the following condition, namely that you no longer spend your time on this quest and search for wisdom, and that if you are caught still doing this, you will die"—if, as I was saying, you were to acquit me on these conditions, I would say to you, "I cherish and love you, men of Athens, but I am more obedient to the god than to you, and so long as I have breath and am able I will not cease seeking wisdom and appealing and demonstrating to every one of you I come across, saying my customary things: Best of men, you are an Athenian, of the greatest and most renowned city in regard to wisdom and power. Are you not ashamed that you care about how you will acquire as much money as possible, and reputation and honor, while you do not care or worry about wisdom and truth and how your soul might be as good as possible?"

c

d

e

And if one of you disputes this and says that he does care, right away I will not let him go or leave him but will question and cross-examine and refute him, and if he does not appear to possess virtue, but he says he does, I will reproach him for considering the most valuable things to be of the least importance and the most worthless to be of the greatest importance. I will do this for anyone I meet, young and old, stranger and citizen, though more for the citizens, insofar as they are closer to me in blood.

30a

Rest assured that the god commands this, and I believe there has never been a greater good for the city than my service to the god. For I go around doing nothing other than persuading you, both young and

old, not to care for your wealth and your bodies ahead of, or as in- b
tensely as, caring for how your soul might be as good as possible, saying that virtue does not come from wealth, but from virtue come
wealth and all other human goods, both private and public. So if I corrupt the young by saying these things, they would be harmful; but if
anyone claims that I say anything different from this, he is talking nonsense. "Men of Athens," I would say, "either be persuaded by Anytus
or not, or acquit me or not, in light of the fact that I would not act dif-
ferently, not even if I am destined to die again and again." c

Do not create a disturbance, men of Athens, but keep to what I
begged of you, not to make a disturbance at what I say and to listen,
since I think by listening you might even be helped. For I am about to
say a few other things to you at which you will perhaps cry out; but
don't do this, no matter what. Rest assured that if you kill me for being
the kind of person I describe, you will not harm me more than yourselves. Neither Meletus nor Anytus can do me any harm; it is not possible, since I think it is not permitted for a better man to be harmed by d
a worse one. Perhaps he will kill or exile or disenfranchise me, but
while he and many others probably think that these are somehow great
evils, I do not. It is a much greater evil to do what this man here is
doing at this moment, attempting to put a man to death unjustly.

Indeed, men of Athens, I am making a defense hardly at all for my
own sake, as one might suppose, but for yours, so you will not commit a wrong concerning the god's gift to you by condemning me. If e
you were to execute me you would not easily find another person like
me, who is—although it is rather funny to say—attached to the city by
the god just as though to a great and noble horse that's somewhat slug-
gish because of its size and needs to be provoked by a gadfly. This is
just the way, I think, the god attached me to the city, the sort of person
who never ceases provoking you and persuading you and reproaching
each one of you the whole day long everywhere I settle. You won't 31a
easily get another person like this, gentlemen, and if you are persuaded
by me, you will spare me. Or, being annoyed just like people roused
from sleep, you might perhaps swat me, and persuaded by Anytus
would put me to death without a second thought. And then you could
live out your days in slumber, unless out of his concern for you the
god sends you someone else.

You can tell from the following that I am the kind of person who is
given by the god to the city: it is not human to disregard all my affairs b
and to endure the neglect of my household for so many years now but
always be acting for your sake, going to each person privately just like
a father or elder brother, urging you to pay attention to virtue. If I had
gained something from these actions and received payment for incit-

ing you in this way, they would make some sense. But you yourselves see now that my accusers, while so shameless in every other charge,

c   lacked the audacity to present a witness to the effect that I ever charged anyone a fee or asked for one. For I believe I provide adequate witness that I am telling the truth: my poverty.

Perhaps it might be thought strange that I go around giving advice and getting myself involved privately, while I do not dare go to our assembly to advise the city publicly. The reason for this is something

d   you have heard me say often and in many places: that something divine and spiritual comes to me, which Meletus jokingly included in the indictment. This has been coming to me as a kind of voice, beginning in childhood, and, whenever it comes, it always diverts me from what I am about to do but never toward anything. This is what prevented me from doing anything political, and I think it was entirely right to oppose me. Rest assured, men of Athens, if long ago I had tried my hand at political matters, long ago I would have perished and

e   benefited neither you nor myself. And do not be offended by my telling the truth; there is no man who could save himself from you or any other populace while honestly opposing you and preventing many un-

32a   just and unlawful things from happening in the city. Rather, someone who genuinely fights for what is just, if he wishes to survive even for a short time, must act privately and not engage in public life.

I will provide you with ample evidence for this—not words, but what you admire, deeds. Listen to what happened to me, so that you may know that I did not yield to anyone, fearing death over justice, even though I might then have lost my life by not yielding. What I will

b   relate is tiresome and lawyerly, but true. I, men of Athens, never held any office in the city apart from being on the council. And it so happened that our tribe, Antiochis, was presiding when you resolved to try as a group—contrary to law, as you all came to realize later—the ten generals[1] who did not rescue the people forsaken in the naval battle. At that time I alone of the committee members was opposed to you doing anything contrary to the laws and I voted against it. With the orators ready to indict and arrest me, and you inciting them and raising

c   a ruckus, I thought it more important for me to risk everything with law and justice on my side than to side with you for fear of imprisonment or death, when you were contemplating unjust actions.

---

1   *the ten generals* After the successful battle of Arginusae, the Athenian generals tasked with retrieving survivors at sea were unable to do so because of a violent storm. Many Athenians were outraged, and the generals were tried as a group and sentenced to death. Socrates opposed the decision on the grounds that Athenian law prohibited a group trial for those accused of a capital crime.

This was when the city was still a democracy. But again, when the oligarchy came to power, the Thirty summoned me and four others into the Rotunda and ordered us to bring Leon the Salaminian[1] from Salamis for execution; they made many such demands of a lot of other people, in order to tarnish as many as possible with their guilt. Then once again I demonstrated, not in speech but in action, that I couldn't care less about death, if it's not too crude to put it that way, but I care the world about this: that I avoid doing anything unjust or unholy. That regime did not intimidate me into doing something unjust, even though it was so powerful. And so when we exited the Rotunda, the other four left for Salamis and brought back Leon, but I left and headed home. And I might have been put to death for this, if the regime had not been overthrown soon after. There are many who will bear witness to these events before you.

Do you think I would have lasted for so many years if I had engaged in politics and, acting in the manner worthy of a good man, I came to the aid of the just decisions and rightly made them my utmost concern? Far from it, men of Athens, and neither would any other man. Throughout my whole life, I have shown myself to be the same sort of man in public—if I did anything at all—as in private, never joining anyone in anything illegal—neither those whom they say—slandering me—are my students, nor anyone else.

I have never been anyone's teacher, but if anybody desired to listen to me talking and fulfilling my mission, whether young or old, I never rejected anyone. Nor do I converse if I receive money but refuse to if I don't, but I allow rich and poor alike to question me, and likewise if anyone wishes to hear whatever I have to say in reply. And if any of them turn out to be good, or not good, I cannot justly be held responsible, since I never promised any instruction to any of them nor did I teach them. And if someone says that he learned anything from me or heard privately something all the others did not hear, rest assured that he is not speaking the truth.

But why then do people enjoy spending a lot of time with me? You have heard why, men of Athens—I told you the whole truth. It is because they enjoy hearing me expose those who think themselves wise but are not, for it is not unpleasant. I was commanded to do this, as I say, by the god, both in oracles and dreams and in every way that any divine fate at all ever ordered a man to do anything whatsoever. This is the truth, men of Athens, and easily tested. Because if I am indeed corrupting some of the young and have corrupted others, then surely if any of them realized when they were older that I recommended

d

e

33a

b

c

d

---

1   *Leon the Salaminian* Leon was an Athenian commander and war hero.

something evil at some point when they were young, they should have come forward just now to accuse me and avenge themselves. If they themselves were reluctant, someone from their family—a father or brother or some other relative—should call it to mind and take revenge, if they ever suffered any evil at my hands.

e   In any case, many of them are present here, whom I can see. First there is Crito here, who is my contemporary and from my district and the father of this man, Critoboulus. Next there is Lysanias of Sphettus, father of Aeschines here. Also, this here is Antiphon of Cephissos, father of Epigenes. These others have brothers who spent their time in this way: Nicostratus son of Theozotides, brother of Theodotus—Theodotus who died, which means that he could not have begged him not to testify—and Paralios here, 'son of Demodocus, whose brother was Theages. And here is Adeimantus, son of Ariston, the brother of Plato here, and Aeantodorus, brother of this man, Apollodorus. I have many others I could mention to you, some of whom Meletus certainly should have brought forth as a witness during his own presentation. If he forgot then, let him call them now—I yield my time—and let him speak if he has anyone of this kind.

34a

Instead you will find the complete opposite of this, gentlemen; they are all ready to help me, the corruptor, the one who harms their kin, as Meletus and Anytus claim. Those who were corrupted perhaps would have a reason to help me. But the uncorrupted, who are already old men and who are their relatives, do they have any other reason for helping me except the right and just one, that they know just as well as Meletus does that he is lying, while I tell the truth?

b

Well then, gentlemen. What *I* would say in my defense is this and maybe other similar points. One of you, perhaps, might then be angry when he is reminded of his own conduct—if, when contesting a lesser charge than this one, he begged and beseeched the judges with many tears, bringing forth his children so that they would pity him even more, with other members of his family and many friends, whereas I will do none of this, even though I run, I might suppose, the ultimate risk. Someone who brought this to mind might be more hard-hearted towards me and, feeling resentful, might cast his vote in anger. If this is really how any of you feel—I don't expect that it is, but if so—it seems reasonable for me to say to that person, "I, Sir, have a family, you know, and was not born 'from oak or from rock'—this is again an expression of Homer[1]—but from human beings, so that I have a family too, and indeed sons, men of Athens, three of them, one already a

c

d

---

1   *an expression of Homer* From *Odyssey* 19.163.

teenager and two who are children. But nonetheless I will not beg you to acquit me by bringing any of them here."

So why then won't I do any of these things? Not out of stubbornness, men of Athens, nor out of disrespect for you. Whether or not I am confident in the face of death is another story, but with respect to my good name, and yours and the whole city's, I don't think it's right for me to do any of these things at my age and with my reputation. Be it true or false, people have at any rate decided that Socrates is superior to most men in some respect, and if any of you who are reputed to be superior in wisdom or courage or any other virtue acted like that, it would be shameful. I have often seen people like this when they are on trial, men of some reputation but carrying on remarkably, as though they thought that something terrible will happen if they die, as if they would be immortal if you did not kill them.

I think these people bring shame upon the city, so that some stranger might think that the foremost of the Athenians in virtue, whom the Athenians nominate ahead of themselves for offices and other honors, they are no better than women. Those of you who are reputed to be something in any way whatsoever, men of Athens, should not do these things, and if we do them you should not permit it but be very clear about it, that you will more readily convict a person who puts on these miserable theatrics and makes a laughingstock of the city than one who holds his peace.

Apart from reputation, gentlemen, I do not think it is right to beg the judges nor to be acquitted by begging, but to teach and persuade instead. The judge does not sit for this reason—to hand out justice as a gift—but for the purpose of judging the case. He did not swear to do favors for whomever he feels like, but to judge according to the laws. We should not accustom you to breaking your oath and neither should you accustom yourselves; neither of us would then be acting piously. Do not, then, men of Athens, expect that I should act towards you in a way that I think is neither fine nor just nor holy, especially when, by Zeus, I am charged precisely with impiety by Meletus here. Clearly, if by begging I persuaded and convinced you who had sworn an oath, I would be teaching you to not believe that the gods exist, and in defending myself I would stupidly be accusing myself of not believing in the gods. But this is not at all how things are, since I do believe in them, men of Athens, unlike all of my accusers. And I trust you and the god to decide my case in whatever way you think is best both for me and for you.

[The judges vote and Socrates is found guilty by 280 votes to 220. The next stage of the trial involves each side proposing a penalty. The prosecution proposes the death penalty. Socrates must respond with a proposal of his own.]

e
36a

Many things contribute to my lack of anger, men of Athens, over what has just happened—that you found me guilty. And I am not surprised that what happened happened. Indeed, I am much more amazed at the final tally of each of the votes, since I, at least, did not think the difference would be so small, but larger. It now appears that if only thirty votes had changed sides, I would have been acquitted. I myself think that I was acquitted of Meletus' charges, and not just acquitted, as it is clear to everyone that if Anytus and Lycon had not joined him in accusing me, he would have owed a thousand drachmas for not receiving a fifth of the votes.[1]

b

The man proposes death as my penalty. Well then. Shall I make a counterproposal to you,[2] men of Athens? Or is it clear what I deserve? What, then? What do I deserve to suffer or pay, knowing that I have not gone about quietly throughout my life but, paying no attention to what the masses care about—money and estate and generalships and political power and other offices and clubs and political parties present in the city—and realizing that in reality I am too honorable a person to pursue these things and survive, I did not pursue the affairs that it would likely have helped neither you nor myself for me to get into, but I set out to accomplish the greatest good, as I declare, by going to each of you privately, trying to persuade each one of you not to put concern for any of his own affairs ahead of concern for how he himself might be as good and wise as possible, nor to put the affairs of the city ahead of the city itself, and to care for other things in the same way—what do I deserve for being such a person? Something good, men of Athens, if I must indeed make a proposal truly in accordance with merit. And more than that, some good which is fitting for me. What then is fitting for a poor man, a benefactor who needs to be at leisure to instruct you? There is nothing more fitting, men of Athens, than to feed such a man in the town hall, even more so than when one of you has won a race at Olympia on a single horse or in a two- or four-horse chariot. For while he makes you think that you are happy,

c

d

---

1   *a fifth of the votes* Because it was considered a matter of public interest to punish impiety, Socrates' accusers would not have had to pay any court fees. To discourage frivolous suits, however, Athenian law levied a substantial fine against plaintiffs who failed to obtain at least one in five of the jury's votes.

2   *Shall I make a counterproposal to you* No penalty was specified by law for some crimes, including the crime of which Socrates has been convicted. Instead, the prosecution and defendant both proposed a penalty and the jurors had to decide which of the two recommended penalties to impose.

I make you so, and while he does not need the nourishment, I do. So e if I must propose a penalty according to justice based on merit, I propose this: dinners in the town hall. 37a

Perhaps in saying this I seem to be speaking to you in much the same way as I spoke about pitying and imploring—out of arrogance. But it is not that, men of Athens, but rather because of the following sort of thing: I am convinced that I wrong no man willingly. But I cannot convince you of this, since we have been talking it over with each other for only a short time, whereas, I think, if your practice was the same as other people's, to deliberate about death penalty cases not just for one day but for many, you would be convinced. But, as it stands, b it's not easy to demolish great prejudices in a short time.

Since I am convinced that I never do wrong, I certainly won't wrong myself and say against myself that I deserve something bad and proposing something of the sort for myself. Why should I? Because I'm afraid of something? So that I can avoid what Meletus proposes for me, when I claim not to know whether it is good or bad? Should I choose something that I am sure is something bad instead of this, and propose it as a penalty? What? Prison? And why must I live in the c prison, enslaved to the Eleven[1] who are appointed to the office at the time? Then how about a fine, with imprisonment until I have paid? But in my case this is the same as what I just said, since I don't have any money to pay with.

Well then, shall I propose exile? You would probably accept this. But I would have an excessive love of life, men of Athens, if I were so stupid that was unable to see that when you, my fellow citizens, could not bear my discussions and speeches, but they became so burden- d some and so resented that you now seek to be free of them—would others willingly put up with them? Far from it, men of Athens. It would be a fine life for me, a man going into exile at my age, to spend my life being driven out and traipsing from one city to another. I'm quite sure that wherever I might go, the young will listen to me speak, just like here. And if I drive them away, they themselves will persuade their elders to drive me away; and if I don't drive them away, their fathers e and relations will do so on their behalf.

Perhaps someone might say, "Can't you live quietly and peacefully in exile, Socrates, for our sake?" This is the hardest thing of all to make some of you believe. For if I say that this would be to disobey the god and so, because of this, I cannot live peacefully, you would think I was being ironic and not believe me. If instead I say that in fact this is the 38a

---

1   *the Eleven* Elected officials in charge of prisons, executions, and confiscations. See *Athenian Constitution* 52.

greatest good for a man, to talk every day about virtue and the other things you hear me converse about when I examine both myself and others, and that the unexamined life is not worth living for a man, you would believe this even less if I said it. As I say, this is how things are, gentlemen; but it is not easy to persuade you.

b   And besides, I am not accustomed to thinking of myself as worthy of anything bad. If I had money, I would have proposed as much money as I could pay, since it wouldn't have harmed me at all. But as it is I can't, unless you are willing to demand of me as much as I can pay. And perhaps I could somehow pay you a mina of silver. So I propose that amount....

Plato here, men of Athens, and Crito and Critoboulus and Apollodorus, they order me to propose thirty minas, and they guarantee it. So I propose that amount, and these men will be dependable guarantors of your silver.

[The jury votes in favor of the death penalty, 360 to 140.]

c   Men of Athens, among those who wish to criticize the city you will gain the reputation and take the blame for putting to death Socrates, a wise man—they will say I am wise, even if I am not, those people who wish to rebuke you—for the sake of a little time, because if you had waited a short while, this would have happened for you of its own accord, since you see that I am already advanced in years and that death is near.

d   I say this not to all of you, but to those who voted to execute me. And I say the following to those same people: perhaps you think, men of Athens, that I was condemned because I lacked the words that would convince you, as if I thought I must do and say everything possible to escape the charge. Far from it. I was condemned by a lack, certainly not of words, but of audacity and shamelessness and by my unwillingness to say to you what would be sweetest for you to hear— me lamenting and wailing and doing and saying many other things

e   that, as I say, are unworthy of me, which you are used to hearing from other people. But I did not think at the time that I must do anything slavish on account of the danger.

Nor do I now regret how I defended myself—I would much rather choose to die having made this kind of defense than live having made

39a   the other kind. Neither on trial nor in war should I or anyone else contrive to avoid death by doing everything possible. Indeed, in battles it often becomes clear that a man could escape death by throwing aside his arms and begging his pursuers for mercy, and there are many other ways of fleeing death in each dangerous situation, provided one has the shamelessness to do and say anything.

It's not that it's not difficult to escape death, gentlemen, but it's much harder to escape wickedness, since it runs faster than death. And now, because I am a slow old man, I am being overtaken by the slower of the two, and my accusers, because they are clever and keen, by the swifter, by evil. And I am going away now, having been condemned to death by you, while they have been condemned by the truth to depravity and injustice. And both I and they will keep to our punishment. Perhaps this is how it had to be, and I suppose it's appropriate.

Next, I want to foretell the future to you my condemners, since I am now at the moment when men especially prophesy: whenever they are about to die. I declare that retribution will come to you swiftly after my death, you men who have killed me, and more troublesome, by Zeus, than the retribution you took when you sentenced me to die. You have done this just now by trying to avoid giving an account of your life, but I think the complete opposite will happen: you will have more prosecutors—whom I was holding back until now, though you did not notice—and as they are younger they will be more troublesome, and you will be more enraged. If you think that killing people will prevent anyone from rebuking you for not living properly, you are not thinking straight, since this escape is scarcely possible nor noble, whereas escape from the other is noblest and easiest: not by cutting down others but equipping oneself so that one can be as good as possible. With this prophecy to you who sentence me, I depart.

I would gladly converse with those who acquitted me, concerning what has come to pass, while the officials are busy and I am not yet on my way to the place where I must die when I arrive. Wait with me, gentlemen, for that long, since nothing prevents us from chatting together while we can. Since you are my friends, I want to show to you the meaning of what has just happened to me.

Something surprising happened to me, judges—and by calling you "judges" I would be using the word appropriately. Always in the past my usual divine prophetic sense was very strong and would even oppose me on detailed points if I was about to do something improper. And what happened to me just now, as you see yourselves, was what people might think, and do think, to be the worst of evils. And yet the sign of the god has not opposed me, not when I left home at dawn, nor when I arrived here in court, nor at any point during my speech when I was about to say something, whereas in many other speeches it has often stopped me, right as I was speaking. But now in this affair it has not been opposed to anything I have said or done.

So what do I take to be the cause of this? I will tell you. There's a good chance that what has happened to me is a good thing and that we understand death incorrectly, those of us who think death is something bad. I have strong evidence for this, since it is impossible that my customary sign would have failed to oppose me, unless I was about to do something good.

Let us also consider how there is great hope that it's a good thing in the following way: Now, death is one of two things, since it's either a kind of not being and the dead person has no perception of anything, or, according to what is said, it is a certain change and migration of the soul from its place here to another place.

d   And if it is the absence of perception and the kind of sleep when someone sleeps without having any dreams, death would be a wonderful gift—because I think if someone had to pick out the night when he slept so soundly that he did not have a dream and compared the other nights and days of his life with this night, and after considering them he had to say how many days and nights he had lived in his life that were better and more sweet than this night, I think that he—not

e   only a private citizen but the great king—would find it easy to count them in comparison with other days and nights. If death is like this, I say it is a gift, since all of time would seem to be nothing more than a single night.

If, in turn, death is a kind of migration from here to another place, and what's said is true and perhaps all of the dead are there, what greater good could there be than this, judges? If someone who arrives

41a   in Hades, having moved on from these so-called judges here, finds those who were truly judges, who are said to act as judges there— Minos and Radamanthus and Aeacus and Triptolemus and as many other demigods who were judges in their own lifetimes—would it be unpleasant to depart? Or to spend time with Orpheus and Musaeus and Hesiod and Homer, how much would any of you give? I am willing to die many times if this is true, since I personally would find life there

b   to be most amazing, if I could meet with Palamedes and Ajax son of Telamon, and anyone of the ancients who died as a result of an unjust decision, and measure my experience against theirs. I think it would not be unpleasant. And the greatest thing would be examining them and finding out which of them is wise and who thinks so but isn't, just like I do to people here.

How much would you give, judges, to quiz the leader of the great

c   army against Troy, or Odysseus, or Sisyphus,[1] or many others one

---

1   *Minos ... Sisyphus* Most of the figures mentioned in this passage are mythological: Minos, Radamanthus, and Aeacus were mortal sons of Zeus, rewarded with the position of judges of the dead because they had established the first just laws on earth; Triptolemus was a demigod who brought agriculture to earth; Orpheus was a singer and a poet, and founder of the Orphic religious cult; Musaeus was a producer of sacred poetry and oracles; Palamedes was a clever inventor; Ajax

might mention, both men and women there whom it would be inde-
scribably marvelous to debate and pass the time with and question? I
should certainly hope that the people there would not put someone to
death for that, since the people there are not just immortal for the rest
of time but happier than those here in other respects, if what is said is
true.

And so you too must be optimistic about death, judges, and hold
this one thing to be true, that for a good man there is nothing evil in   d
either living or dying. And neither do his deeds go unnoticed by the
gods. My actions just now did not happen by themselves, but it is clear
to me that it was to my advantage to die now and be released from my
troubles. Because of this, my sign never deterred me. And I am not at
all angry at those who voted against me and not much at my accusers—though they did not vote against me or accuse me with this in
mind, but instead did so intending to harm me, and they deserve to be   e
blamed for this.

Nonetheless, I beg them for this much: revenge yourselves on my
sons, when they have grown, gentlemen, by giving them the same trouble I gave you, if they seem to prioritize money or anything else ahead
of virtue or if they think themselves to be something that they are not.
Reproach them as I reproached you, for not caring about what they
ought to and for thinking that they are something when they are worth
nothing. If you would do this, I will have been served justice by you,   42a
and my sons, too.

But now it really is time to depart, I to die and you to go on living.
But which of us goes to a better life is unclear to everyone except to
the god.

---

was a king and Greek hero in the Trojan War; Odysseus was a cunning and eloquent Greek hero of the Trojan War, and protagonist of the *Odyssey*; Sisyphus
was a king punished in the underworld by having perpetually to push a rock up-
hill. Possibly real figures were two revered Greek poets: Homer, author of the
Iliad and the *Odyssey*, and Hesiod, whose only surviving works are *Works and
Days* and the *Theogony*.

Crito

Introduction

In this dialogue, which takes place while Socrates is in prison awaiting execution, one of his best friends, Crito, tries to persuade him to escape while Socrates gives his reasons for refusing to do so.

Ancient Greek executions normally took place only a day or two after conviction, but Socrates' death was unusually delayed for religious reasons. No executions were permitted while the city was purified for the annual holy festival for the god Apollo—the god, incidentally, who is described in the *Apology* as having given Socrates his divine mission through the oracle at Delphi. The dates of this festival were marked by the departure and return of a special holy ship that traveled between Athens and Apollo's sacred island of Delos. The ship had left Athens the day before Socrates' trial and normally would have been gone for a couple of weeks, but this year contrary winds kept it away for thirty days. For this reason, Socrates had not only a month to languish in prison—where he was kept in chains overnight to discourage his escape—but also extra time to indulge in his favorite activity: having philosophical discussions with his friends.

The main topic of the *Crito* is whether it is ever permissible to do anything unjust. Socrates argues that it would be unjust for him to disobey the laws of Athens, and that therefore he will not do so on this occasion, even though on the face of it doing so would be in his own interests (and would benefit others and cause no one any particular harm).

Crito

Socrates: Why have you come at this hour, Crito? Or isn't it still early? 43a

Crito: It certainly is.

Socrates: About what time is it?

Crito: Just before dawn.

Socrates: I'm surprised that the prison guard was willing to let you in.

Crito: He is used to me by now, Socrates, since I visit here so often. And besides, I have done him a good turn.

Socrates: Did you get here just now or a while ago?

Crito: Quite a while ago.

b   Socrates: So how come you didn't wake me up immediately, but sat by in silence?

Crito: By Zeus, no, Socrates. I wish I myself were not so sleepless and sorrowful, and so I have been marveling at you, when I see how peacefully you've been sleeping. I deliberately didn't wake you so that you would pass the time as peacefully as possible. And indeed, many times before I have thought you fortunate in your demeanor towards your entire life, and even more so in your present misfortune, so easily and calmly do you bear it.

Socrates: It's because it would be out of tune, Crito, to be angry, at my age, if I must finally die.

c   Crito: And yet others of your age, Socrates, have been caught up in such misfortunes, but their age does not prevent them from being angry at their fate.

Socrates: That's true. But why did you come so early?

Crito: Carrying troubling news, Socrates—though not for you, as it appears—but deeply troubling for me and all of your friends, and I, it seems, am among the most heavily burdened.

d   Socrates: What is it? Has the ship arrived from Delos, upon whose arrival I must die?

Crito: No, it hasn't arrived, but it looks like it will arrive today, based on the report of some people who have come from Sounion[1] and who left when it was there. It's clear from this that it will arrive today, and you will have to end your life tomorrow, Socrates.

Socrates: May it be for the best, Crito. If this pleases the gods, so be it. However, I don't think it will come today.

Crito: Where do you get your evidence for this?   44a

Socrates: I will tell you. I must be put to death sometime the day after the ship arrives?

Crito: That's what the authorities in these matters say, at least.

Socrates: In that case, I don't think it will arrive this coming day, but the next. My evidence is something I saw in a dream a little while ago during the night. It's likely that you chose a very good time not to wake me.

Crito: Well, what was the dream?

Socrates: A woman appeared, coming towards me, fine and good-look-   b
ing, wearing white clothing. She called to me and said, "Socrates, you shall arrive in fertile Phthia on the third day."[2]

Crito: What a strange dream, Socrates.

Socrates: But obvious, at least as it appears to me, Crito.

Crito: Too obvious, perhaps. But, my supernatural Socrates, even now listen to me and be saved. If you die, for me it won't be just one mis- fortune: apart from being separated from the kind of friend the like of which I will never find again, many people, moreover, who do not know me and you well will think that I could have saved you if I were   c
willing to spend the money, but that I didn't care to. And wouldn't this indeed be the most shameful reputation, that I would seem to value money above friends? For the many will not believe that it was you

---

1   *Sounion* The tip of Attica; a headland 200 feet above sea level, bearing a temple to Poseidon, where ships headed for Athens could be sighted early.

2   *fertile Phthia ... third day* In the *Iliad* 9.363, Achilles threatens to leave Troy and return home, saying "in three days shall I be in Phthia."

yourself who refused to leave here, even though we were urging you to.

Socrates: But why, blessed Crito, should we care so much about the opinion of the many? The best people, who are more deserving of our attention, will believe that the matter was handled in just the way it was.

d   Crito: But surely you see, Socrates, that we must pay attention to the opinion of the many, too. The present circumstances make it clear that the many can inflict not just the least of evils but practically the greatest, when one has been slandered amongst them.

Socrates: If they were of any use, Crito, the many would be able to do the greatest evils, and so they would also be able to do the greatest goods, and that would be fine. But as it is they can do neither, since they cannot make a man either wise or foolish, but they do just whatever occurs to them.

e   Crito: Well, let's leave that there. But tell me this, Socrates. You're not worried, are you, about me and your other friends, how, if you were to leave here, the informers would make trouble for us because we stole you away from here, and we would be compelled either to give up all our property or a good deal of money, or suffer some other punish-
45a   ment at their hands? If you have any such fear, let it go, because it is our obligation to run this risk in saving you and even greater ones if necessary. So trust me and do not refuse.

Socrates: I certainly am worried about these things, Crito, and lots of others too.

Crito: Well don't fear them. Indeed, some people only need to be given a little silver and they're willing to rescue you and get you out of here. And on top of that, don't you see how cheap those informers are and
b   that we wouldn't need to spend a lot of money on them? My money is at your disposal, and is, I think, sufficient. Furthermore, even if, because of some concern for me, you think you shouldn't spend my money, there are these visitors here who are prepared to spend theirs. One of them has brought enough silver for this very purpose, Simmias of Thebes, and Cebes too is willing, and very many others. So, as I say, don't give up on saving yourself because you are uneasy about these things.

And don't let what you said in the court get to you, that you would-
n't know what to do with yourself as an exile. Wherever you go, there
are places they will welcome you. And if you want to go to Thessaly,   c
I have some friends there who will think highly of you and provide
you with safety, so that no one in Thessaly will harass you.

What's more, Socrates, what you are doing doesn't seem right to
me, giving yourself up when you could be saved, ready to have happen to you what your enemies would urge—and did urge—in their
wish to destroy you.

I also think you are betraying your sons, whom you could raise and   d
educate, by going away and abandoning them, and, as far as you are
concerned, they can experience whatever happens to come their way,
when it's likely that as orphans they'll get the usual orphans' treatment
of orphans. One should either not have children or endure the hardship
of raising and educating them. But it looks to me as though you are taking the laziest path, whereas you must choose the path a good and
brave man would choose, especially when you keep saying that you
care about virtue your whole life long.

So I am ashamed both on your behalf and on behalf of us, your   e
friends, that this whole affair surrounding you will be thought to have
happened due to some cowardice on our part: the hearing of the
charge in court, that it came to trial when it need not have,[1] and the
legal contest itself, how it was carried on, and, as the absurd part of
the affair, that by some badness and cowardice on our part we will be
thought to have let this final act get away from us, since we did not   46a
save you, nor you save yourself, when it was possible and we could
have done so if we were of the slightest use. So see, Socrates, whether
this is both evil and shameful, for you and for us as well. Think
over—or rather, there's no longer time for thinking but only for de-
ciding—this one consideration, because everything must be done this
coming night; if we hang around any longer it will be impossible and
we'll no longer be able to. So in every way, Socrates, believe me and
do not refuse.

Socrates: My dear Crito, your eagerness would be worth a lot if it were   b
in pursuit of something righteous, but the more it is not, the more difficult it is to deal with. We must therefore examine whether we should
do this or not, because as always, and not just now for the first time, I
am the sort of person who is persuaded in my soul by nothing other

---

1   *when it need not have* Socrates could have left the country and so avoided the
    trial.

than the argument which seems best to me upon reflection. At present I am not able to abandon the arguments I previously made, now that this misfortune has befallen me, but they appear about the same to me, and I defer to and honor the ones I did before. If we have nothing better than them to offer under the present circumstances, rest assured that I will not agree with you, not if, even more so than at present, the power of the multitude were to spook us as though we were children, imposing chains and deaths and monetary fines upon us.

What's the most reasonable way we can examine this matter? By first resuming this argument that you give about reputations. Was it correct on each occasion when we said that one must pay attention to the opinions of some people and not to others'? Was this the correct thing to say before I had to die, whereas now it has become obvious that it was said only for the sake of argument and was actually just child's play and hot air?

I am determined to examine this together with you, Crito, whether it appears different when I consider it in this condition, or the same, and whether we should ignore it or be persuaded by it. It is always put like this, I think, by people who think there is something in it, the way I put it just now: that it is necessary to pay serious attention to some of the opinions that men hold and not to others. By the gods, Crito, doesn't this seem correct to you? Because you, as far as any human can tell, are in no danger of being executed tomorrow and the present misfortune should not lead you astray. Have a look, then. Is it fair enough to say that one should not value every human opinion but only some and not others? And not the opinions of everyone but of some and not others? What do you say? Isn't this right?

Crito: Yes, that's right.

Socrates: Shouldn't we value the good opinions, and not the worthless ones?

Crito: Yes.

Socrates: Aren't the good ones the opinions of the wise, while the worthless ones come from the ignorant?

Crito: Of course.

Socrates: So then, what did we say, again, about cases such as this: should a man in training, who takes it seriously, pay any heed to the praise and blame and opinion of everyone, or only to one person, the one who is a doctor or a trainer?

Crito: Only to the one.

Socrates: So he should fear the criticisms and welcome the praises of that one person, and not those of the many?

Crito: Clearly.

Socrates: He must practice and exercise, and eat and drink, in the way that seems best to that one person, the trainer and expert, more than to all the others together.

Crito: That's right.

Socrates: Well then. If he disobeys this one man and dishonors his opinion and his praises and instead honors those of the many who know nothing, won't he suffer harm?   c

Crito: How could he not?

Socrates: What is this harm, and what does it tend to do, and in what part of the disobedient person?

Crito: It's clear that it's in the body, since this is what it destroys.

Socrates: Well said. Isn't it the same with the other things—not to go over them all, but in particular justice and injustice and shameful and fine things and good and bad, which are what our current discussion is about—whether we must follow the opinion   d
of the many and fear it or instead the opinion of the one person, if there is someone who has knowledge, whom we must defer to and fear more than all the others together? If we do not heed his opinion we will corrupt and harm that part of us which becomes better with justice and is destroyed by injustice. Or don't you think so?

Crito: I do indeed, Socrates.

Socrates: Tell me, if we do not follow the opinion of the person who knows and so destroy that part of us which is improved by what is

e   wholesome and corrupted by what sickens, is life worth living when
that part is ruined? This is the body, I suppose, isn't it?

Crito: Yes.

Socrates: Then is life worth living with a wretched and corrupt body?

Crito: Not at all.

Socrates: And is life worth living after the part of us which injustice
injures and justice benefits has been corrupted? Or do you think this
is unimportant in comparison with the body, this part of us, whatever
48a   it is, that injustice and justice affect?

Crito: Not at all.

Socrates: But more valuable?

Crito: Much more.

Socrates: So, best of men, we must not pay much heed to what the
many will say to us, but to what the one who knows about just and unjust things will say—to that one person, and to the truth itself. So you
were wrong, at the beginning, to bring this up, that we must heed the
opinion of the many concerning just things and noble things and good
things and their opposites. "But in spite of that," someone might declare, "the many can put us to death."

b   Crito: That too is obvious. For someone might say so, Socrates. You're
right.

Socrates: But, you wonderful fellow, it seems to me that the following
statement, which we have been over before, remains just the same as
before. So examine again whether or not it still holds true for you, that
it's not living that should be our priority, but living well.

Crito: Why, of course it's still true.

Socrates: And that this is living well and finely and justly, does that remain true or not?

Crito: It remains true.

Socrates: Therefore, based on what you've agreed, we must consider the following: whether it is just or unjust for me to try to leave here, when I was not acquitted by the Athenians. And if it seems just let's try it, and if not, let's abandon it. As for the points you make about spending money and reputation and the upbringing of children, Crito, I suspect that these are really questions belonging to people who would casually put someone to death and resurrect him, if they could, without any thought—to the members of the multitude.

c

As for us, since the argument requires it, I suppose we should examine precisely what we just mentioned: whether we will act justly by giving money and thanks to those who will get me out of here—both you in the lead and me being led—or whether we will in fact act unjustly by doing all of this. If we think that we're acting unjustly by doing these things, I don't think we should take into consideration whether we will die if we hold our ground and keep our peace, or anything else we will suffer—only whether we're acting unjustly.

d

Crito: I think you put that well, Socrates. See what we should do, then.

Socrates: Let's look together, my good man, and if at any point you have an objection to what I am saying, make it and I will persuade you; if not, you blessed man, finally quit saying the same thing over and over, that I have to get out of here against the will of the Athenians. I think it is most important to act with your consent and not against your will. See, then, that the starting point of the inquiry is laid down to your satisfaction and try to answer the questions in the way you think best.

e

49a

Crito: I shall certainly try.

Socrates: Do we say that we should never willingly act unjustly, or that we should in some instances and not in others? Or is acting unjustly never good or noble, as we often agreed on previous occasions? Or have all our previous agreements been overturned in these last few days, and did we fail to notice long ago, Crito, that when we have serious discussions with one another, we ourselves, at our age, are no different from children? Or more than anything isn't what we used to say still true? Whether the many agree or not, and whether we must also suffer harsher things than these or gentler, nevertheless acting unjustly is evil and shameful in every way for the person who does it. Do we say this or not?

b

Crito: We do.

Socrates: And so one must never act unjustly.

Crito: By no means.

Socrates: And so one should not repay an injustice with an injustice, as the many think, since one should never act unjustly.

c   Crito: It appears not.

Socrates: What next? Should one cause harm, Crito, or not?

Crito: Presumably not, Socrates.

Socrates: And then? Is returning a harm for a harm just, as the many say, or not just?

Crito: Not at all.

Socrates: Because harming a man in any way is no different from doing an injustice.

Crito: That's true.

Socrates: One must neither repay an injustice nor cause harm to any man, no matter what one suffers because of him. And see to it, Crito, d   that in agreeing with this you are not agreeing contrary to what you believe, because I know that few people believe it or will believe it. And so there is no common ground between those who hold this belief and those who don't; when they see each other's positions they are bound to despise one other. So think carefully about whether you yourself agree and believe, and let us begin thinking from here: that it is never right to act unjustly, or to return an injustice, or to retaliate when one has suffered some harm by repaying the harm. Do you reject or accept e   this starting principle? For it still seems good to me now, as it did long ago, but if it seemed some other way to you, speak up and educate me. If you're sticking to what we said before, listen to what comes next.

Crito: I do stick to it, and I accept it. Go ahead.

Socrates: Here in turn is the next point. Or rather, I'll ask you: when someone has made an agreement with someone else, and it is just, must he keep to it or betray it?

Crito: He must keep to it.

Socrates: Observe what follows from this. If we leave here without having persuaded the city, are we doing someone a harm—and those 50a whom we should least of all harm—or not? And are we keeping to the just agreements we made, or not?

Crito: I'm unable to respond to what you're asking, Socrates; for I do not know.

Socrates: Well, look at it this way. If the laws and the community of the city came to us when we were about to sneak away from here—or whatever it should be called—and, standing over us, were to ask, "Tell me, Socrates, what are you intending to do? By attempting this deed, aren't you planning to do nothing other than destroy us, the laws, and b the civic community, as much as you can? Or does it seem possible to you that any city where the verdicts reached have no force but are made powerless and corrupted by private citizens could continue to exist and not be in ruins?"

What will we say, Crito, to these questions and others like them? Because there's a lot more a person could say, especially an orator, on behalf of this law we're destroying, which makes sovereign the verdicts that have been decided. Or will we say to them, "The city treated c us unjustly and did not decide the case properly"? Will we say this or something like it?

Crito: By Zeus, that's what we'll say, Socrates.

Socrates: What if the laws then said, "Socrates, did we agree on this, we and you, to honor the decisions that the city makes?" And if we were surprised to hear them say this, perhaps they would say, "Socrates, don't be surprised at what we're saying, but answer, since you are accustomed to using questions and answers. Come then, what reason can you give us and the city for trying to destroy us? Did we not, to begin with, d give birth to you? And wasn't it through us that your father married your mother and conceived you? So show those of us, the laws concerning marriages, what fault you find that keeps them from being good?" "I find no fault with them," I would say.

"What about the laws concerning the upbringing and education of children, by which you too were raised? Or didn't those of us, the laws established on this matter, give good instructions when they directed your father to educate you in the arts and gymnastics?" "They did," I would say.

e

"Well, then. Since you have been born and brought up and educated, could you say that you were not our offspring and slave from the beginning, both you and your ancestors? And if this is so, do you suppose that justice between you and us is based on equality, and do you think that whatever we might try to do to you, it is just for you to do these things to us in return? Justice between you and your father, or your master if you happened to have one, was not based on equality, so that you could not do whatever you had suffered in return, neither speak back when crossed nor strike back when struck nor many other such things. Will you be allowed to do this to your homeland and the laws, so that, if we try to destroy you, thinking this to be just, you will in return try to destroy us the laws and your homeland with as much power as you have and claim that you're acting justly in doing so—the man who truly cares about virtue?

51a

"Are you so wise that it has slipped your mind that the homeland deserves more honor and reverence and worship than your mother and father and all of your other ancestors? And that she is held in higher esteem both by the gods and by men of good sense? And that when she is angry you should show her more respect and compliance and obedience than your father, and either convince her or do what she commands, and suffer without complaining if she orders you to suffer something? And that whether it is to be beaten or imprisoned, or to be wounded or killed if she leads you into war, you must do it? And that this is just, and that you must not be daunted or withdraw or abandon your position, but at war and in the courts and everywhere you must do what the city and the homeland order, or convince her by appealing to what is naturally just? And that it is not holy to use force against one's mother or father, and it is so much worse to do so against one's homeland?" What will we say to this, Crito? That the laws speak the truth? Or not?

b

c

Crito: It looks so to me.

Socrates: "Consider, then, Socrates," the laws might say, "if what we say is true: that it is not just for you to try what you're now attempting to do to us. For we gave birth to you, brought you up, educated you, and gave you and all the other citizens every good thing we could, and yet even so we pronounce that any Athenian who wishes, once he has been admitted as an adult and sees the affairs of the city and us the laws, has the power, if he is not pleased with us, to take his possessions

d

and leave for wherever he wants. And if any among you wants to live in a colony because we and the city do not satisfy him, or if he wants to go somewhere else and live as a foreigner, none of us laws stands in the way or forbids him from taking his possessions with him and leaving for wherever he wants.

"But whoever remains with us, having observed how we decide lawsuits and take care of other civic matters, we claim that this man by his action has now made an agreement with us to do what we command him to do, and we claim that anyone who does not obey is guilty three times over: he disobeys us who gave birth to him; and who raised him; and because, despite agreeing to be subject to us, he does not obey us or persuade us that we are doing something improper. And we give him an alternative and don't angrily press him to do what we order; and although we allow either of two possibilities—either to persuade us or to comply—he does neither of these.

"We say that you especially will be liable to these charges, Socrates, if indeed you carry out your plans, and you not least of the Athenians but most of all." If, then, I would say, "How do you mean?", perhaps they would scold me justly, saying that I most of all among the Athenians have made this agreement. They might say, "Socrates, we have great evidence for this, that we and the city satisfy you. For you would never have spent more of your life here than all of the other Athenians unless it seemed particularly good to you. You never left the city for a festival, except once to the Isthmus, but never went anywhere else except on military duty, nor did you ever make another trip like other Athenians do, nor did any urge seize you to get to know a different city or other laws, but we and our city were sufficient for you. So decidedly did you choose us and agree to be governed by us that, among other things, you had children in it, because the city was satisfactory to you.

"Moreover, at your trial you could have proposed exile, if you had wished, and what you're now trying to do to the city without her consent, you could have done then with her consent. At the time, you prided yourself on not being angry if you had to die, and you chose death, you said, in preference to exile. But now you neither feel shame in the face of those words nor have you any respect for us the laws. By trying to destroy us you are doing what the most despicable slave would do, trying to run away contrary to the contract and the agreement by which you agreed to be governed by us. So answer us first on this particular point: do we speak the truth when we say that you agreed to be governed by us in deed and not merely in words?" What can we say to this, Crito? Mustn't we agree?

Crito: We must, Socrates.

e   Socrates: "Aren't you," they might say, "going against your contracts and agreements with us, which you were not forced to agree to, nor deceived about, nor compelled to decide upon in a short time, but over seventy years, in which time you could have gone away if we did not satisfy you and these agreements did not appear just to you. You did not prefer Lacedaemon[1] or Crete, each of which you claim is well-governed,

53a   nor any of the other Hellenic cities or the foreign ones, but you left her less often than the lame and the blind and the other disabled people. Evidently the city and also we the laws were so much more pleasing to you than to other Athenians, for is a city pleasing to anyone without its laws? Now then, won't you keep to what you agreed? You will, if you are convinced by us, at any rate, Socrates; and at least you won't make yourself ridiculous by leaving the city.

"Just think about what good will it do you and your friends if you break them and do wrong in one of these ways. It's pretty clear that your

b   friends will risk exile along with you and disenfranchisement from the city and confiscation of their property. And if you first go to one of the closest cities, to Thebes or to Megara—since both are well-governed— you will come as an enemy, Socrates, of those governments, and everyone who cares about their cities will regard you suspiciously, thinking that you are a destroyer of the laws.[2] And you will confirm the opinion of

c   the judges, so that they will think they judged the case correctly, since whoever is a destroyer of the laws would certainly be considered in some way a destroyer of young and foolish men.

"Will you flee, then, from well-governed cities and from the most civilized people? Is it worth it to you to live like this? Will you associate with them, Socrates, and feel no shame when talking with them? What will you say, Socrates? What you said here, that virtue and justice are of the greatest value to humans, and along with lawfulness and the laws? And you don't think the conduct of such a Socrates will ap-

d   pear shameful? One should think so.

"But will you leave these places and go to Crito's friends in Thessaly.[3] There is plenty of disorder and disobedience there and they might listen with pleasure to you, about how you amusingly ran away from prison wearing some costume or a peasant's vest or something else of the sort that runaways typically dress themselves in, altering your appearance. But still, will no one say that an old man, who probably only has a short time left in his life, was so greedy in his desire to live that

e   he dared to violate the greatest laws? Perhaps not, if you do not annoy anyone. But if you do, Socrates, you will hear many dishonorable things about yourself. You will surely spend your life sucking up to

---

1   *Lacedaemon* Sparta.

2   *Thebes or to Megara ... destroyer of the laws* These were oligarchical states neighboring Athens. Socrates would be seen as an enemy because he was a lawbreaker.

3   *Thessaly* The Athenians associated this place with gluttony and debauchery.

everyone and living like a slave. What else will you do in Thessaly but feast, as though you had traveled to Thessaly for dinner? And those speeches, the ones about justice and the other virtues, where will they be?   54a

"Is it for the sake of your children that you want to live, so that you can raise and educate them? What are you going do, in that case? You'll raise and educate them by bringing them to Thessaly and making them outsiders, so that they will enjoy that benefit too? Or if not that, will they grow up better if they are raised and educated with you away from them but alive, because your friends will take care of them? But is it that if you go to Thessaly, they'll look after them, whereas if you go to Hades, they won't? If those who claim to be your friends are any good, you must believe they will.   b

"So be convinced by us who brought you up, Socrates, and do not put children or life or anything else ahead of justice, so that when you go to Hades you will be able to provide all this as your defense to those who rule there. Since neither in this world, nor in the next when you arrive, will this action be thought better or more just or more pious for you and your friends to do. But as it is you leave us, if indeed you depart, having been done an injustice not by us, the laws, but by men. If   c you return the injustice, however, and repay the harm and flee in shame, having violated your agreement and contract with us and harmed those who least of all should be harmed—yourself, your friends, your homeland, and us—we will make life hard for you while you're alive, and then our brothers, the laws in Hades, will not receive you favorably, knowing that you tried to destroy us too, as far as you were able. So do not be persuaded by Crito to do what he says instead   d of what we say."

Rest assured, my dear friend Crito, that this is what I seem to hear, just as the Corybants[1] seem to hear the pipes, and the echo from these words resonates within me and makes me unable to hear anything else. So know that, based on my current beliefs, at least, if you speak against them you will speak in vain. Nevertheless, if you honestly think you can achieve anything more, speak.

Crito: No, Socrates. I am unable to speak.

Socrates: Then let it be, Crito, and let us act in this way, since this is   e where the god leads us.

---

1   *Corybants* Priests of the Asiatic goddess Cybele. The rites of the Corybants were accompanied by wild music and dancing.

Death Scene from *Phaedo*

Introduction

This dialogue is set sometime after Socrates' death. Phaedo, one of Socrates' younger friends, is depicted as describing his final hours to a group in Phlius, a Greek city that was allied with Sparta. The complete dialogue includes the description of a long discussion between Socrates and his visitors about what happens to the soul after death—indeed, the dialogue was originally known as *On the Soul*. At the beginning of the dialogue, preceding this discussion, is a description of the ideal life, and the dialogue concludes with a speculative account of the passage of the soul to the afterlife, which includes a theory of the structure of the earth and its regions.

The only part of the dialogue that is excerpted here, however, is the final scene: a description of Socrates' words and demeanor as he carries out his own execution by drinking a cup of poison. There has been much debate as to whether a potion of hemlock would have the relatively peaceful lethal effects that are depicted here; it used to be thought that Plato was using poetic license, but recent research[1] suggests that the particular species of hemlock found near ancient Athens would in fact have acted in just the way that Plato describes.

from *Phaedo*

"... A man ought to be confident about his soul if, during his life, he has shunned glamorous things and the other pleasures of the body, considering them foreign to him and causing more harm than good, but instead has devoted himself to the pleasures of learning. And having beautified his soul with nothing but its own adornments—namely self-control and justice and courage and freedom and truth—in this state he

114e

115a

1   See Enid Bloch, "Hemlock Poisoning and the Death of Socrates: Did Plato Tell the Truth?" *The Trial and Execution of Socrates*, ed. T.C. Brickhouse and N.D. Smith (Oxford: Oxford UP, 2001), pp. 255–78.

awaits his journey to Hades, prepared to go whenever fate calls. So while you," he said, "Simmias and Cebes and you others, will each make this journey later when his time comes, fate is now, as a trage-dian would say, already calling me, and it is nearly time that I go to the bath, because I think it is clearly better to bathe myself before drink-ing the poison and save the women the trouble of bathing a corpse."

b   When he said this Crito asked, "Well then, Socrates, do you have any final requests for these men or myself, concerning your children or anything else, which we could do for you and so be of some par-ticular service to you?"

"The things I always say, Crito," he replied. "Nothing very new. By taking good care of yourselves you are of service to me and my family as well as yourselves, no matter what you do, even if you don't think so at present. But if you neglect yourselves and are unwilling to live, as though following tracks, in accordance with what we now say and have said in the past too, then you will accomplish next to

c   nothing, no matter how much or how earnestly you agree with me at present."

"We will certainly be eager to act in this way," he replied. "But how should we bury you?"

"However you want to," he responded, "if you can actually catch me and I don't escape you." And laughing quietly he turned to face us and said, "Men, I can't convince Crito that I am this man Socrates who is speaking right now and arranging each of his sentences. Instead, he

d   thinks I am what he will shortly see as a corpse, and so he asks how he should bury me. And what I have been going on about at length— about how, after I drink the poison I will no longer be with you but will have departed, on my way to the particular joys of the blessed—it seems I was saying these things to him for some other reason, to en-courage you and myself at the same time.

"So give Crito a guarantee for me," he said, "the opposite guaran-tee to the one he gave the judges; for his was that I would stay, but

e   you must guarantee him that I won't stay when I die, but will go away and leave, so that Crito will more easily bear it and won't be angry on my behalf, as if I am suffering something terrible, when he sees my body being burned or buried, nor say at my funeral that *Socrates* is being laid out, or carried out, or buried. For rest assured, great Crito," said he, "speaking poorly is not only discordant in itself, but also causes some harm to souls. But you must be brave and say that you will

116a   bury my body, and bury it in whatever manner you like and as you think is customary."

Having said this he set off to bathe in another room, and Crito fol-lowed him, but he ordered us to stay behind. So we stayed, talking amongst ourselves about what had been said and re-examining it, and then returned to dwell on how great a misfortune had befallen us, thinking that since we were being deprived of a father, we would literally be spending life hereafter as orphans.

When he had bathed and his children had been brought in—he had   b
two small sons and one older one—and the women of the family had come and he had spoken to them in Crito's presence and instructed them as he wanted, he ordered the women and children to leave and joined us. It was already close to sunset, for he had spent a long time inside. He came from his bath and sat down and didn't say much more after that. The servant of the Eleven came and, standing next to him, said, "Socrates, I won't observe from you the behavior I see from oth-   c
ers, who are angry with me and curse me when, on the orders of the magistrates, I tell them to drink the poison. This whole time I have found you in other ways to be the most noble and kind and best man of those who have ever come here. And so I am sure that now too you will be angry not with me but with those others, since you know who is responsible. So now, since you know what I have come to tell you, farewell, and try to bear what must be as easily as possible." And he   d
cried as he turned and left.

And Socrates looked in his direction and said, "Farewell to you too. We will do it." And then to us he said, "How polite the man is. Throughout this whole time he has come to check on me and sometimes talked with me and was as kind as could be, and how genuinely he weeps for me now.

"But come on, Crito, let's obey him. Have someone bring in the poison, if it has been ground. If not, have the man grind it."

And Crito said, "But I think there is still sun on the mountains,   e
Socrates, and it is not quite sunset. And I know that others have taken the poison very late, after the order has been given to them, eating and drinking exceedingly well and having sex, some of them, with people they love. So don't hurry. There is still time."

And Socrates said, "The people who act in this way, the ones you mention, Crito, act reasonably because they think it will benefit them to do such things. But I will be reasonable by not doing them. For I think that drinking a little later will bring me nothing except to make   117a
me ridiculous in my own eyes, clinging to life and being thrifty with it when there's nothing left in it. So come, obey me and don't do otherwise."

And Crito heeded him and nodded to the boy who had been standing nearby, and the boy went out. After a long time had passed he came back leading the man who was to present the poison, which was ground up in a cup he was carrying. Seeing him, Socrates said, "Well then, best of men, since you are the expert in these matters, what should I do?"

b
"You only have to drink it," he said, "and walk around until you feel your legs become heavy. Then lie down, and from there it will work on its own." And at the same time he handed the cup to Socrates.

And taking it very good-naturedly, Echecrates,[1] without fear and without changing color or expression, he looked at the man as would a bull and said, "What do you say about pouring out an offering to a god from the drink? Is it allowed, or not?"

"We only prepare as much as we think is needed, Socrates," he said.

c
"I understand," said he. "But surely it is permissible, and necessary, to pray to the gods, that my migration from here to there will be blessed. So I pray for this, that it will happen in this way." And as he said this he raised the cup and drank it down, very gently and calmly.

Until then the majority of us had been able to keep ourselves from crying reasonably well, but when we saw him drinking, and then that he had finished it ... no longer. And my own tears poured out of me with the force of a flood, and I hid myself in shame and cried for my-

d
self—for truly I was crying not for him but for my own misfortune, that I was being deprived of such a comrade. Crito had turned away even before I did, when he was unable to restrain his tears. Apollodorus had been crying the entire time, and when he howled with grief and anger at this particular moment, nobody who was present could help breaking down, except Socrates himself.

And he said, "What a way to behave, you remarkable men! I sent the women away mainly for this reason, so that they would not make such an offensive sound, because I have heard that one must meet

e
one's end in calmed silence. So be quiet and collect yourselves." And when we heard this we were ashamed and ceased crying.

He was walking around, and when he said his legs had become heavy, he lay down on his back—since this was what the man had instructed—and the man who had given him the poison took hold of him, and after a while examined his feet and legs and then squeezed his foot hard and asked if he felt it. He said that he didn't. After this,

118a
the man squeezed his calves, and going higher in this way he showed us that he was cold and congealed. Socrates grasped himself and said that when it reached his heart, he would be gone.

And then when nearly all of the area around his belly was growing cold, he uncovered his head, for he had covered it, and said—he ut-

---

1   *Echecrates* Pythagorean philosopher, to whom this narrative is being addressed. Most of what we know about him comes from the *Phaedo*.

tered his final words—"Crito," he said, "we owe a cock to Asclepius.[1] Make the offering and don't forget."

"It will be done," Crito said. "But see if you have anything else to say."

He said nothing further in response to the question, but after a short time he shuddered. The man uncovered him. His eyes were fixed. And Crito, seeing this, closed his mouth and eyes.

This, Echecrates, is how our friend passed away, a man who, we would say, was the best of those we have ever known, and the wisest and most just.

---

1   *a cock to Asclepius* A sacrifice of a cockerel to the god of medicine and healing. The command "Make the offering and don't forget" is in the second person plural.

Bibliography

Adam, J., ed. *Platonis Apologia Socratis*. Cambridge: Cambridge, 1887.

——, ed. *Platonis Crito*. Cambridge: Cambridge, 1888.

——, ed. *Platonis Euthyphro*. Cambridge: Cambridge, 1890.

Aristotle. *Athenian Constitution*. Trans. Sir Frederic G. Kenyon. London: G. Bell, 1914.

Burnet, John, ed. *Euthyphro, Apology of Socrates, Crito*. Oxford: Clarendon, 1924.

Duke, E.A., W.F. Hicken, W.S.M. Nicoll, D.B. Robinson, and J.C.G. Strachan, eds. *Plato Opera Volume I: Euthyphro, Apologia, Crito, Phaedo, Cratylus, Theaetetus, Sophista, Politicus*. Oxford: Clarendon, 1995.

Dyer, Louis, ed. *Apology of Socrates and Crito*. Boston: Ginn & Company, 1895.

Flagg, Isaac, ed. *Plato the Apology and Crito*. New York: American Book Company, 1907.

Graves, C.E., ed. *The Euthyphro and Menexenus of Plato*. London: Macmillan, 1881.

Heidel, William Arthur, ed. *Plato's Euthyphro*. New York: American Book Company, 1902.

Helm, James J., ed. *Apology*. Mundelein: Bolchazy-Carducci, 1997.

Stanford, Charles Stuart, ed. *Plato's Apology of Socrates, Crito, and Phaedo.* London: Simpkin and Marshall, 1834.

Tyler, W.S., ed. *Plato's Apology and Crito, New Edition*. New York and London: D. Appleton, 1872

Wagner, W., ed. *Plato's Apology of Socrates and Crito*. Boston: John Allyn, 1877.

Wells, G.H., ed. *The Euthyphro of Plato*. London: George Bell and Sons, 1880.

Index

From the Publisher

A name never says it all, but the word "Broadview" expresses a good deal of the philosophy behind our company. We are open to a broad range of academic approaches and political viewpoints. We pay attention to the broad impact book publishing and book printing has in the wider world; we began using recycled stock more than a decade ago, and for some years now we have used 100% recycled paper for most titles. Our publishing program is internationally oriented and broad-ranging. Our individual titles often appeal to a broad readership too; many are of interest as much to general readers as to academics and students.

Founded in 1985, Broadview remains a fully independent company owned by its shareholders—not an imprint or subsidiary of a larger multinational.

For the most accurate information on our books (including information on pricing, editions, and formats) please visit our website at www.broadviewpress.com. Our print books and ebooks are also available for sale on our site.

On the Broadview website we also offer several goods that are not books—among them the Broadview coffee mug, the Broadview beer stein (inscribed with a line from Geoffrey Chaucer's *Canterbury Tales*), the Broadview fridge magnets (your choice of philosophical or literary), and a range of T-shirts (made from combinations of hemp, bamboo, and/or high-quality pima cotton, with no child labor, sweatshop labor, or environmental degradation involved in their manufacture).

All these goods are available through the "merchandise" section of the Broadview website. When you buy Broadview goods you can support other goods too.

broadview press
www.broadviewpress.com